Advanced Praise for
Bankruptcy Preference Clawbacks in Plain English

"Jones' book is an essential tool used in my practice. Its place is on my desk right next to the Bankruptcy Code."
—JACK FUERST, ESQ.

"Roland has crafted a great primer for creditors facing the complex world of preferences in Bankruptcy, an area that you don't wade into alone."
—GRAIG CORVELEYN, ESQ.

"A great resource for the client, and the lawyer too."
—SCOTT SCHIFF, ESQ.

"This fascinating book is useful for both lawyers and businesspeople. Roland Jones has kept faith with his title and taken on the difficult task of explaining the esoteric, but important subject of bankruptcy preference law with lively and jargon-free writing and brilliant examples. Further, the book is packed with valuable practical suggestions for almost any situation which may arise in a case, as well as helpful legal precedents. And the writing is so much more interesting, fun and dynamic than other legal writing."
—ERIC HABER, ESQ.

"The definitive source for understanding and defending preference litigation."
—JIM TOBIA, ESQ.

"Roland has stripped down the complexity of clawbacks, while providing a comprehensive analysis of all issues. Excellent read."
—NICK RIGANO, ESQ.

"Roland Jones is the gold standard in bankruptcy clawback lawsuits. Wherever you may be in the USA, Jones will know the details of your local rules, the ins and outs of the bar, whether to go soft or scorched earth and how you can get out of this jam with the lowest possible costs. These are hard cases because the law seems terribly unfair, but Jones and his team make the whole process much easier. I've known him for almost 20 years and he's my number one choice in making bankruptcy clawback referrals."
—RON DRESCHER, ESQ.

Bankruptcy Preference Clawbacks
in Plain English

Bankruptcy Preference Clawbacks in Plain English

Why They Exist.

How to Defend Yourself.

Roland Gary Jones, Esq.

Pelican Bay Press

Pelican Bay Press

10 9 8 7 6 5 4 3 2 1
First English Edition 2018

ISBN 13: 978-0-9851173-0-6

Cover and book design by CenterPointe Media
www.CenterPointeMedia.com

DEDICATION

To my wife, Nance, and my daughter, Katherine.

Table of Contents

Table of Contents

CHAPTER 1

Introduction and Structure of Book

1.1   What Is a Preference Clawback Lawsuit?

A preference clawback lawsuit is a case brought by a trustee,[1] creditors' committee,[2] or debtor[3] under section 547 of the United States Bankruptcy Code.[4] The lawsuit seeks to prove that a creditor[5] received preferential payments[6] during the 90-day period before the debtor filed for bankruptcy.

---

1. "The representative of the bankruptcy estate who exercises statutory powers, principally for the benefit of the unsecured creditors, under the general supervision of the court and the direct supervision of the U.S. trustee or bankruptcy administrator. The trustee is a private individual or corporation appointed in all chapter 7, chapter 12, and chapter 13 cases and some chapter 11 cases. The trustee's responsibilities include reviewing the debtor's petition and schedules and bringing actions against creditors or the debtor to recover property of the bankruptcy estate. In chapter 7, the trustee liquidates property of the estate, and makes distributions to creditors. Trustees in chapter 12 and 13 have similar duties to a chapter 7 trustee and the additional responsibilities of overseeing the debtor's plan, receiving payments from debtors, and disbursing plan payments to creditors." United States Courts, *Bankruptcy Basics Glossary*, http://www.uscourts.gov/educational-resources/educational-activities/bankruptcy-basics-glossary.

2. A committee composed of the 20 largest unsecured creditors. *See* 11 U.S.C. § 1102 ("Creditors' and equity security holders' committees"); *see also* Kenneth N. Klee & K. John Shaffer, *Chapter 11 Issues: Creditors' Committees Under Chapter 11 of the Bankruptcy Code*, 44 S.C. L. Rev. 995, 1003 (1993) (stating that "the U.S. Trustee typically makes its committee selections from a list of the twenty largest creditors filed by the debtor at or near the commencement of the case pursuant to Rule 1007(d) of the Federal Rules of Bankruptcy Procedure").

3. "A person who has filed a petition for relief under the Bankruptcy Code." United States Courts, *Bankruptcy Basics Glossary*, http://www.uscourts.gov/educational-resources/educational-activities/bankruptcy-basics-glossary.

4. "The informal name for title 11 of the United States Code (11 U.S.C. §§ 101-1330), the federal bankruptcy law." *Id.*

5. "One to whom the debtor owes money or who claims to be owed money by the debtor." *Id.*

6. "A debt payment made to a creditor in the 90-day period before a debtor files bankruptcy (or within one year if the creditor was an insider) that gives the creditor more than the creditor would receive in the debtor's chapter 7 case." *Id.*

Once preferential treatment is established, the bankruptcy judge will order the preferred creditor to return all preferential payments.[7]

1.2   Why I Wrote This Book

I have defended bankruptcy preference clawback cases for over 20 years. Every client wants to know three things:

- Why am I being sued?

- What are my defenses?

- What will happen in my case?

I wrote this book to try to answer those questions.

1.3   The Structure of the Book

- First, I will explain the problem that the preference laws try to fix.

- Second, I will describe the defenses to a preference lawsuit.

- Third, I will introduce you to the leading players in a typical case.

- Fourth, I will set out the timeline of a case.

- Fifth, I will show that the preference laws are ineffective, and suggest how they could be improved.

---

7. 11 U.S.C. § 547.

CHAPTER 2

Why Am I Being Sued?

2.1 Preface

A trustee or other plaintiff is suing you because an insolvent debtor paid you in full *before* bankruptcy while other creditors who were paid *after* the bankruptcy likely will receive a tiny percentage of what they are owed or nothing. It's unfair for a debtor to play favorites (or "*prefer*" certain creditors) by paying some creditors in full while leaving other creditors holding the proverbial bag.

The preference laws attempt to remedy this unfairness by forcing folks who got special treatment to return the money. These creditors will now get paid whatever creditors in the same class get paid. Instead of full payment, they will probably receive a small percentage of their claims from the debtor's post-bankruptcy assets.

Not all "preferred" creditors must return money to the trustee. Some creditors can keep their preferential payments. Creditors that can hold on to their payments are those creditors that had no special knowledge and took no particular action to get paid during the preference period. They were "preferred" by accident. These creditors may be granted immunity to the trustee's clawback efforts.

2.2   A Debtor and Two Creditors—Moe, Larry, and Curly

Moe borrows $10,000 each from Larry and Curly. Moe repays Curly $10,000 (all the money he has), pays Larry nothing, and files for bankruptcy a week later. Moe had nothing left after paying Curly, so Larry gets nothing in the bankruptcy. The bankruptcy trustee wants to do his job of splitting up Moe's assets fairly, but Moe has no assets left after paying Curly. The trustee sues Curly to get back the $10,000 paid to Curly so he can divide the money equitably between Larry and Curly.

Let's break down what just happened.

- Moe paid Curly before a bankruptcy.

- Moe paid Curly in full. Curly gets 100 cents on the dollar.

- Moe paid Curly in full when he didn't have the money to pay both Curly and Larry in full. In fact, he paid all his money to Curly.

- A week later, after a bankruptcy, Larry gets 0 cents on the dollar.

- The trustee sues Curly to get back the $10,000.

2.3   The Creditor Conflict

- Larry says: "It's not fair that Moe had a limited amount of money but paid it all to Curly instead of dividing it evenly between Curly and me."

- Curly says: "Larry is not my problem. I got paid back what I was owed fair and square. It's not fair to grab *my* money back. I am not responsible for Larry getting paid."

2.4   Irreconcilable Differences

It's a problem that we can view from two justifiable perspectives.

First perspective: bankruptcy is supposed to treat all creditors fairly in the division of the debtor's assets.[8] If a debtor pays his assets out to a

---

8. *See* Michael J. Herbert, *The Trustee Versus the Trade Creditor II: The 1984 Amendment to Section 547(c)(2) of the Bank-*

sweetheart creditor before the bankruptcy, he short-circuits the purpose of the bankruptcy laws.[9] Also, paying one creditor and not paying other creditors is not fair to the other creditors.[10]

Second perspective: As a creditor, I have the absolute right to collect as much as I am legally owed. Of course, I'm going to try even harder to collect if I think a debtor is about to go bankrupt. It's not my job or responsibility to worry about whether other creditors will get paid.[11]

Conclusion:

- It's unfair for some creditors to end up with no payment or little payment when a debtor is paying other creditors in full on the eve of bankruptcy.[12]

- It's also unfair to force innocent creditors who were rightfully paid on valid debts to pay back what is now their money.[13]

The two perspectives cannot be reconciled.

Welcome to the little problem that has stumped lawmakers for the past 500 years. It seems that unfairness to one creditor is inevitable.

---

ruptcy Code, 2 Bank. Dev. J. 201, 203 (1985) (stating there are "two goals of bankruptcy law: discouraging the creditors from racing to the courthouse, and treating the creditors equally") (citing 2 *Norton Bankr. L. & Prac. § 32.01 (1981)*); Bethaney J. Vazzana, *Trustee Recovery of Indirect Benefits Under Section 547(b) of the Bankruptcy Code*, 6 Bank. Dev. J. 403, 403 (1989) (stating that Congress drafted bankruptcy statutes "with the intention of promoting efficiency in bankruptcy cases, assuring equality among similarly situated creditors").

9. Beverly J. Hall, *Recent Developments in Bankruptcy Law: Preferences and Setoffs: Sections 547 and 553*, 2 Bank. Dev. J. 49 (1985) ("[A] preference is a showing of favoritism toward certain creditors."); *In re* Arctic Air Conditioning, Inc., 35 B.R. 107 (Bankr. E.D. Tenn. 1983) (stating that repayment of loans during 90-day pre-petition period constitutes avoidable transfer where such payments diminish the debtor's assets that would have been available to all creditors); *see also* Charles Jordan Tabb, *Panglossian Preference Paradigm?* 5 Am. Bankr. Inst. L. Rev. 407, 409 (1997) ("Prebankruptcy transfers of an insolvent debtor's property enable preferred creditors to recover more than their fair share of the debtor's insufficient pie—more than if the transfer had not been made.").

10. *Id.*; Hall, *supra* note 9, at 50 (stating that preferring a creditor is "objectionable because assets are diminished which otherwise would be available for distribution to all creditors") (citing Report on Bankruptcy Laws, H.R. Doc. No. 137, 93rd Cong., 1st Sess. 170, 202 (1973)).

11. Tabb, *supra* note 9, at 408 (stating that outside of bankruptcy, "first in time, first in right . . . [p]references in payment are perfectly permissible"); *id.* at 409-10 ("The fact that an insolvent debtor made a transfer to a creditor shortly before bankruptcy . . . is not enough, standing alone, to warrant avoidance and recapture."); *see also* Herbert, *supra* note 8, at 203 (stating that creditors would engage in prebankruptcy "racing to the courthouse").

12. *See* Tabb, *supra* note 9, at 409.

13. *Id.* at 410 ("For centuries, a creditor who simply got paid for an outstanding debt did nothing wrong, and in the interest of repose and justice, was allowed to keep the payment.").

Any solution that alleviates the injustice for one creditor just creates unfairness for the other creditor, like a seesaw.

2.5   The Old Solution

In seventeenth-century England, judges tried to fix this problem by distinguishing bad preference recipients from good preference recipients:[14]

- Good (or "accidental") preference recipients were creditors who were minding their own business, conducting business as usual, and just happened to get paid in full by an insolvent debtor before a bankruptcy.[15]

- Bad preference recipients were creditors who actively conspired to get paid in full on the eve of a bankruptcy, intentionally leaving all others with the short end of the stick.[16]

Bad creditors were bad in the above scenario because they knew about the impending bankruptcy and intentionally schemed to get an advantage.[17]

---

14. David A. Ontko, *Ordinary Business Terms Must Not Be Ignored: The [F]orgotten But Critical Role of § 547(c)(2)(c) in the Ordinary Course of Business Exception to the Preference Rules*, 6 Bank. Dev. J. 429, 431 (1989) ("The ability to avoid payments between debtors and creditors in a commercial setting first arose under the English fraudulent conveyance doctrine during the late 1500's.").

15. *Id.* at 432 ("Both English law and the Act, therefore, protected the majority of normal business payments between debtors and creditors unless the trustee could affirmatively demonstrate bad faith on the part of one of the parties."); *see also* Tabb, *supra* note 9, at 410 ("For centuries, a creditor who simply got paid for an outstanding debt did nothing wrong, and in the interest of repose and justice, was allowed to keep the payment.").

16. Thomas H. Jackson, *Avoiding Powers in Bankruptcy,* 36 Stan. L. Rev. 725, 758 (1984) (stating that outside of bankruptcy, creditors race for debtors' assets to prevent being left with nothing); *see also* Tabb, *supra* note 9, at 410 ("Creditors, knowing that the debtor was in financial distress, would race to dismember the debtor, grabbing whatever assets they could, and consequently driving the debtor out of business and eliminating any chance for the troubled debtor to recover financially.").

17. Ontko, *supra* note 14, at 432 (noting that "the creditor's state of mind became the focus"); Cohen v. Kern (*In re Kennesaw Mint, Inc.*), 32 B.R. 799, 804 (Bankr. N.D. Ga. 1983) (stating that to avoid a preference, trustees had to "prove the creditor ha[d] reasonable cause to believe the debtor was insolvent"); Jackson, *supra* note 16, at 759 (stating that creditors who knew of debtors' inevitable insolvency attempted to receive payments prior to bankruptcy to avoid being placed in parity with other unsecured creditors).

2.5.1   A Tale of Two Curly's

- Bad Curly. The "bad" Curly calls Moe to collect his debt. He finds out Moe is about to file for bankruptcy. Curly and Moe decide to cut Larry out. They agree that Moe will pay Curly $10,000 and then file for bankruptcy in a week, leaving Larry with nothing.

- Good Curly. The "good" Curly has no clue Moe is in financial trouble and just happens to get a check for $10,000 in the mail from Moe before the bankruptcy. He is shocked and outraged when the trustee sues to take it away from him.

Under the old law, what mattered was what a creditor knew and intended.[18] But trustees found it hard to prove what a creditor knew or was thinking unless he admitted it.[19] As a result, trustees clawed back few preferential payments.[20]

In our example, the trustee would have to prove that Curly *intended* to get ahead of other creditors and *knew* about Moe's coming bankruptcy. Good luck with that, Mr. Trustee!

Since trying to prove what was in a creditor's mind was so difficult, trustees won very few clawback cases.[21]

2.6   1978—The Preference Laws Rewritten

Fast-forward 500 years.

---

18. Ontko, *supra* note 14, at 432 (noting that "the creditor's state of mind became the focus"); *see also In re* Kennesaw Mint, Inc., 32 Bankr. at 804 (stating that to avoid a preference, trustees had to "prove the creditor had reasonable cause to believe the debtor was insolvent").

19. Ontko, *supra* note 14, at 432 (stating there was a "burden placed on the trustee to prove both the debtor's insolvency and creditor's knowledge of preferential treatment"); Barash v. Public Fin. Corp., 658 F.2d 504, 510 (7th Cir. 1981) (stating that "trustees rarely sought recovery because of the difficulty of proving insolvency").

20. Ontko, *supra* note 14, at 432 ("Though focusing on the mindset of a different party to establish avoidability, the presumption still favored upholding transfers . . . thus protecting most ordinary course payments which would normally not create a suspicion of insolvency."); *see also id.* ("Current expenses, incurred in what might be termed the ordinary course of business, were seldom avoidable . . . due to the burden placed on the trustee to demonstrate creditor knowledge . . . .").

21. Id. at 433 (stating that requiring the trustee "to prove both debtor insolvency at the time of the transfer and creditors' knowledge of the insolvency and possible preference, prevented the trustee from avoiding transfers") (citing Report of the Commission on the Bankruptcy Laws of the United States, H.R. Doc. No. 137, 93d Cong., 1st Sess. pt. I, at 202 (1973)).

In the 1970s, law professors from places like Harvard and Stanford took up the fight for downtrodden trustees. They started sending down legal articles from ivory towers urging lawmakers to fix the preference laws.[22]

2.6.1 News Flash—Intent Not Important—Equal Treatment in Bankruptcy Is What It's About!

The professors decided that bankruptcy's highest priority should be that all creditors get treated equally. Since the existing preference laws were letting some creditors get away with preferential treatment, Congress must revise them. The stumbling block was the laws' sticky intent requirement. The professors decided to get rid of intent altogether.

The bow ties proposed the following solution—

- First, a trustee would no longer need to prove preferential intent.[23]

- Second, the law would deem *all* payments preferential and subject to clawback if made 90 days before bankruptcy and the debtor was insolvent.[24]

- Third, Congress would create a safe harbor for deserving creditors. These creditors, *even though they were preferred*, would be safe from the trustee's clawback clutches.[25]

Congress enacted these ideas into law as part of the Bankruptcy Reform Act of 1978.[26]

---

22. Troy A. McKenzie, *Judicial Independence, Autonomy, and the Bankruptcy Courts*, 62 Stan. L. Rev. 747, 758 (2010) ("By the 1970s, criticism of the bankruptcy process was widespread in academic and policymaking circles." (citing David A. Skeel, Jr., *Debt's Dominion: A History of Bankruptcy Law in America* 136-47 (2001))).

23. Hall, *supra* note 9; *see also Barash*, 658 F.2d at 510 (stating that "creditor's knowledge or state of mind is no longer relevant"); *id.* (stating that "the 1978 amendments . . . eliminated the reasonable-cause-to-believe element and established the presumption of insolvency").

24. Hall, *supra* note 9, at 80 (citing 11 U.S.C. § 547(f), which states, in part, "[T]he debtor is presumed to have been insolvent on and during the 90 days immediately preceding the date of the filing of the petition, making all transfers conveyed on the 'eve' of bankruptcy inherently suspect.").

25. Herbert, *supra* note 8, at 203 (stating that the law "provides protection for transfers made in the ordinary course of the debtor's financial or business affairs"); *see also* 11 U.S.C. § 547(c)(2).

26. Pub. L. 95-598, 92 Stat. 2549, November 6, 1978.

2.6.2 The Insolvency Presumption[27]

In addition to abolishing the intent requirement, Congress created a presumption that the debtor was insolvent during the 90-day period before the bankruptcy.[28] Now trustees didn't have to prove insolvency—Congress removed another impediment to their clawback efforts.[29]

2.6.3 Winning Is Easy!

Bankruptcy trustees suddenly found it much easier to win preference cases.[30] They only needed to prove that:

- the debtor paid the money during the 90-day preference period,[31]

- the creditor got the money, and[32]

---

27. Section 547(b) sets out the entire burden of the trustee. It states:
   (b) Except as provided in subsections (c) and (i) of this section, the trustee may avoid any transfer of an interest of the debtor in property—
   (1) to or for the benefit of a creditor;
   (2) for or on account of an antecedent debt owed by the debtor before such transfer was made;
   (3) made while the debtor was insolvent;
   (4) made—
      (A) on or within 90 days before the date of the filing of the petition; or
      (B) between ninety days and one year before the date of the filing of the petition, if such creditor at the time of such transfer was an insider; and
   (5) that enables such creditor to receive more than such creditor would receive if—
      (A) the case were a case under chapter 7 of this title;
      (B) the transfer had not been made; and
      (C) such creditor received payment of such debt to the extent provided by the provisions of this title

28. 11 U.S.C. § 547(f); Brian S. Goldstein, *Recent Development in Bankruptcy Law: Preferences and Setoff*, 1 Bank. Dev. J. 356, 360 (1984) ("The trustee is aided in his proof that the transfer was made while the debtor was insolvent by a statutory presumption that the debtor was insolvent 90 days prior to the filing of his petition"); *see also* Hall, supra note 9, at 80 (citing 11 U.S.C. § 547(f), which states, in part, "[T]he debtor is presumed to have been insolvent on and during the 90 days immediately preceding the date of the filing of the petition, making all transfers conveyed on the 'eve' of bankruptcy inherently suspect.").

29. Hall, *supra* note 9, at 52 ("The trustee has the burden of establishing each element by a preponderance of the evidence, except for proving the debtor's insolvency. The debtor is presumed to be insolvent . . . .").

30. Tabb, *supra* note 9, at 418 ("Trustees can bring blanket preference actions against every unsecured creditor who got paid within the ninety days before bankruptcy, without bothering to investigate the 'ordinariness' of any specific payment."); *see also* Hall, supra note 9, at 79 (citing 11 U.S.C. § 547(f), which states, in part, "The purpose of this presumption [of debtor insolvency] is to simplify the trustee's burden of proof by eliminating an initial necessity of reconstructing the debtor's financial condition.").

31. *Id.* at 59 ("The transfer must have been made within ninety days prior to the petition's filing, unless made to an 'insider.'"); *see also* 11 U.S.C. § 547(b)(4).

32. Hall, *supra* note 9, at 52-53 ("Three tests must be met in order for this element to be satisfied: (1) the transfer must have occurred; (2) the transfer must have involved the debtor's property or an interest in the debtor's property; and (3)

- the creditor would have been paid less in the bankruptcy.[33]

The Bankruptcy Code now pretty much assumes that *all* payments made in the 90-day period are preferential and subject to clawback.[34] Creditors must successfully assert a "safe harbor" defense or return the payments.[35]

So, in 1978, Congress scrapped 500 years of carefully circumscribed clawback laws and gave Trustees new laws with much sharper claws.[36]

Of course, enthusiastic trustees began suing every creditor they could find who received payments in the preference period.

This practice continues to this day.

2.7   The Defenses—Guilty with an Explanation

It bears repeating that since 1978, there is likely no question that you received a preference. If you got paid in the 90-day period when the debtor was insolvent before filing for bankruptcy, you most likely got a "preferred" payment.

The good news is that being preferred does not necessarily result in a clawback. You have defenses.

Since many bankruptcy creditors are now deemed "guilty" of having been preferred, the defenses to a clawback are really "explanations"

---

the transfer must have been made to or for a creditor's benefit."); *see also* 11 U.S.C. § 547(b).

33. Hall, *supra* note 9, at 65-66 ("The transfer must have enabled the creditor to receive more than would have been received if . . . the transfer had not been made . . . ."); *see also* 11 U.S.C. § 547(b)(5).

34. *Barash*, 658 F.2d at 509 (stating that the preferred creditor must always disgorge all preferential transfers it received); *see also* 11 U.S.C. § 547(b)(4)(A).

35. Evan C. Hollander, *Recent Development: Preferences: Section 547*, 3 Bank. Dev. J. 365, 365 (1986) ("In order to combat a preference action, a defendandcreditor [sic] must prove either that one of the subsection (b) requirements is lacking, or that the transaction fits into one of the disjunctive exceptions to avoidability found in Section 547(c) of the Bankruptcy Code."); *see also* Hall, *supra* note 9, at 50 (explaining that once the presumption is established, "the burden shifts to the creditor who must prove that the transfer should be excepted from avoidance").

36. Vern Countryman, *The Concept of a Voidable Preference in Bankruptcy*, 38 Vand. L. Rev. 713, 726 (1985) ("The draftsmen of the Bankruptcy Reform Act of 1978 addressed . . . preferential transfers by almost entirely eliminating any requirement that the creditor have reasonable cause to believe the debtor insolvent"); Lawrence Ponoroff, *BAPCPA AT TEN: Bankruptcy Preferences: Recalcitrant Passengers Aboard the Flight from Creditor Equality*, 90 Am. Bankr. L.J. 329, 331 (2016) ("the Bankruptcy Reform Act of 1978 was unquestionably the most debtor-friendly U.S. bankruptcy law ever enacted . . . ."); Herbert, *supra* note 8, at 205 (1985) ("Unfortunately for these creditors, the payments by the debtor on the old debt are often preferential transfers.").

excusing a preferred creditor from returning the payment. Thus, I call the defenses "guilty-with-an-explanation" defenses.

I describe the major defenses in Part 3 below.[37]

2.8   Rationales for the Preference Laws

When defending yourself against a preference clawback, it helps to know the law's justifications so you can argue why they don't apply in your case.

Judges often recite these boilerplate rationales when approving preference clawbacks. [38] It reminds me of my father taking me to the woodshed and explaining why it was good for me. I can't help but sense a little defensiveness. But don't blame the judges—blame Congress.

The typical rationales for the preference clawback laws are that the laws:

- result in a fairer distribution to creditors,[39]

- discourage aggressive creditors in the pre-bankruptcy period,[40]

- help troubled debtors,[41] and

- encourage more transparency.[42]

---

37. Herbert, *supra* note 8, at 203 (1985) ("Congress also established a number of statutory exceptions to the voidability of preferential transfers.").

38. Thomas Ross, *The Impact of Section 547 of the Bankruptcy Code upon Secured and Unsecured Creditors,* 69 Minn. L. Rev. 39, 45 (1984) (explaining that preference laws can be "justified by several policies"); *see also* Lawrence Ponoroff & Julie C. Ashby, *Desperate Times and Desperate Measures: The Troubled State of the Ordinary Course of Business Defense – and What to Do About It,* 72 Wash. L. Rev. 5, 43 (1997) (stating that there are "multiple interpretations" for determining applicable industry standards).

39. Ross, *supra* note 39, at 45 (stating that preference law "facilitates a more equal distribution of the debtor's property" to creditors); *see also* Ilan Markus, *The Correct Application of Section 547(e)(3): Deciding Whether Wage Garnishment Transfers Are Preferential,* 12 Bank. Dev. J. 219, 223 (1995) (stating that preference laws "facilitate the prime bankruptcy policy of equality of distribution among creditors of the debtor").

40. *Id.* (stating that preference law "discourages the dismemberment of ailing, but salvageable, debtors. When creditors are grabbing for their piece of a debtor, a debtor's recovery can be foreclosed. The specter of preference discourages grabbing and facilitates a debtor's recovery." (citing Grant Gilmore, *Security Interests in Personal Property* § 8.3, 257-261 (1965))).

41. *Id.*

42. Jonathan C. Lipson, *The Shadow Bankruptcy System,* 89 B.U. L. Rev. 1609, 1620 (2009) ("[I]n 1978, Congress created a system that it believed would maximize transparency. Transparency would, in turn, increase recoveries and confidence in the system through informed stakeholder control.").

2.8.1   The Preference Laws Result in a Fairer Distribution

Let's go back to our example. Moe, who is insolvent, owes both Larry and Curly but pays all his money to Curly. Larry gets nothing in the bankruptcy.

An obvious reason for the preference laws is to foster equality of treatment.

In theory, the bankruptcy trustee sues Curly, gets back the big payment, puts it in a pot, and distributes it to both Larry and Curly equally.

If this happened in practice, the rationale would hold water.

Unfortunately, the reality is different. The trustee might recover money from Curly. However, the trustee does not put those dollars into a "pot" for unsecured creditors. She commingles that money with other funds. The trustee pays estate expenses with the clawed-back cash. Clawback money may go to pay the debtor's lawyers, secured creditors, ongoing costs like electricity and water, and, last but not least, the lawyers who sued to claw back the money.

If the bankruptcy estate is administratively insolvent, Larry may very well get *none* of Moe's preferential payment to Curly. "Administratively insolvent" means that the assets of the business are not enough to pay the estate expenses and priority creditors. In this case, the clawback money will be siphoned off to pay expenses and priority creditors. There will be nothing left to pay unsecured creditors like Larry.

If the estate is solvent, unsecured creditors might get paid. However, the amount they get paid is not in direct proportion to how much the trustee clawed back. Clawback income is not segregated. Payments to unsecured creditors is merely a function of what is left over after paying higher priority creditors.

Money clawed back from Curly so that Larry could share equitably with Curly is not set aside for Larry and Curly. So Larry does not necessarily get paid any of the money that was clawed back from Curly.

In fact, Larry may not only not get more money—since he may get none of the clawback money—but may end up getting *less* money than before the clawback.

"How is this possible?" you ask.

Here you go.

- First, the trustee takes Curly's money and spends it on "administrative expenses."

- Second, Curly gets a *new* claim against the bankruptcy estate for the debt that is now unpaid, since the trustee has clawed back the money that paid that debt.

- Third, Larry must *now* share any money available to unsecured creditors with Curly.

- Remember, the trustee didn't put Curly's money in the pot, so he didn't add any new money—*but he added one more person to share in the pot*, i.e., Curly.

- So, Larry would get a smaller distribution thanks to the clawback lawsuit—the clawback lawsuit that was meant to help Larry. This would occur since the money that eventually trickles down to unsecured creditors is often not enough to offset further division of the funds by new (clawed back) creditors.

Given the significant administrative costs in every case and the number of creditors ranked above and paid before unsecured creditors I doubt that anything near 100% of the clawback cash ever trickles down to the unsecureds.

No one knows for sure.

The clawback laws don't require the trustee to set aside those clawback bucks for unsecured creditors.[43] Also, the relevant records are difficult

---

43. Harstad v. First Am. Bank, 39 F.2d 898, 905 (8th Cir. 1994) (finding that a trustee is not required to demonstrate a direct benefit to creditors from preference recovery); *see also* Countryman, *supra* note 37, at 824 (citing Thomas Jackson, *Avoiding Powers in Bankruptcy*, 36 Stan. L Rev. 725 (1984), and stating that according to Professor Jackson, the purpose of preference laws "is not to preserve the bankruptcy distribution policy but to punish culpable creditors").

or impractical to obtain. Bankruptcy is a fishbowl but a very cloudy one when it comes to how trustees allocate clawback money.

2.8.2 Discourages Aggressive Creditors in the Prebankruptcy Period (Nope)

Another common rationale I call the "Moby Dick rationale" because it assumes that creditors are like sharks taking bites out of a dying whale.

The theory is that clawback laws are useful because they stop creditors from acting aggressively against a flailing debtor. The logic is that creditors will eschew preferential payments because they will have to return the money later.[44]

The logic is flawed.

First, a creditor has zero reason to expect a bankruptcy filing merely because a customer is paying slowly. Companies often pay late. That doesn't mean they are about to file for bankruptcy. Even the most sophisticated creditors may be clueless as to when, or if, a debtor is going to file for bankruptcy.[45]

Only creditors with crystal balls (or inside information) know for sure that they are getting paid in the 90-day preference period.

Even if a creditor knew that he would be later sued for a clawback, that would not stop him from trying to get paid now. He would simply grab as much as possible now and fight to keep as much as possible later.[46]

---

44. Grant Gilmore, *Security Interests in Personal Property* § 8.3, 257-61 (1965) (stating that preference law "discourages the dismemberment of ailing, but salvageable, debtors. When creditors are grabbing for their piece of a debtor, a debtor's recovery can be foreclosed. The specter of preference discourages grabbing and facilitates a debtor's recovery.").

45. Countryman, *supra* note 37, at 729-30 (stating that as a result of creditor's inability to know when a debtor will file for bankruptcy, "[o]ne consequence of the [1978] Reform Act changes, as the reported cases reveal, has been that, in most cases, the creditor-defendant in a preference action makes no effort to rebut the section 547(f) presumption of the debtor's insolvency within the ninety day prebankruptcy period, and the presumption carries the day for the trustee or other party attacking the preference on the insolvency issue").

46. Tabb, *supra* note 9, at 411 ("Even though there is a possibility of recapture of a preference, seeking the preference may still be to the creditor's advantage."); *see also* John C. McCoid, II, *Bankruptcy, Preferences, and Efficiency: An Expression of Doubt*, 67 Va. L. Rev. 249, 264 (1981) (explaining that even if a preference is recaptured, the asset in the creditor's hands for that period may have produced income greater than that owed under the recapture).

No sane creditor would hold back collecting payment in full because he *might* have to give some of the money back two years later.[47]

2.8.3 Helps Troubled Debtors (No, They Don't)

This rationale presumes that the clawback laws discourage aggressive creditors and therefore give the debtor breathing space to recover financially.[48] The reality is that not only do these laws do nothing to deter creditors (as seen above), they *hasten* bankruptcy filings.[49] As discussed in Part 3 below, giving the debtor longer terms may destroy a significant defense to a preference lawsuit.[50] The preference laws generally punish any attempt to work out a payment plan right before bankruptcy. Since payment plans can be a critical factor in stabilizing a teetering company, the structure of the preference laws makes bankruptcies more likely.[51] Of course, since no creditor can predict precisely when a bankruptcy will occur, some brave creditors will continue to help debtors *despite* the preference laws.[52]

---

47. Tabb, *supra* note 9, at, 411 (1997) ("The only sanction for seeking a preference is that the 'offending' creditor will have to give the money back with interest."); *see also* Brian S. Goldstein, *Recent Development in Bankruptcy Law: Preferences and Setoff,* 1 Bank. Dev. J. 356, 357 (1984) (citing *In re* Gander Mountain, Inc., 29 Bankr. 260 (Bankr. E.D. Wis. 1983) (holding that the creditor's right to set off the dividend that would be received in a preferential transfer is limited to instances where (1) the preferred creditor is entitled to receive dividends, (2) dividends can be quickly and easily ascertained, and (3) the dividend is immediately payable)).

48. Tabb, *supra* note 9, at 410 (stating that without preference laws, "[c]reditors, knowing that the debtor was in financial distress, would race to dismember the debtor, grabbing whatever assets they could, and consequently driving the debtor out of business and eliminating any chance for the troubled debtor to recover financially").

49. Herbert, *supra* note 8, at 206 (stating that "any action of the seller taken to induce payment is sufficient to render the transfer not in the ordinary course of business . . . even a unilateral action by the buyer changing the terms of its payment may be sufficient to preclude immunization of the transfer under Section 547(c)(2)").

50. *Id.; id.* at 207 (noting a "lack of flexibility" in comparing previous creditor-debtor relationship activity with activity during the preference period); *see also* Robert Weisberg, *Commercial Morality, the Merchant Character, and the History of the Voidable Preference,* 39 Stan. L. Rev. 3, 12 (1986) ("Perhaps no aspect of the landmark 1978 Bankruptcy Code has displayed such a pretense to scientific formalism as section 547, which purported to be the final scientific word on preferences, a radically systematic scheme of definition and exception.").

51. *Id.* at 205 (stating that "the trade creditor who receives payments under a workout may be forced to return some or all of the payments received to the bankrupt debtor's estate").

52. *Id.* (stating that although the preference laws provide creditors with a disincentive to deal because of the risk of eventual non-payment, "to the extent trade creditors are aware of preference exceptions, and are able to use them creatively to prevent subsequent avoidance of preferential transfers, this disincentive is reduced"); Weisberg, *supra* note 52, at 135 ("No creditor taking a transfer can know at the time he receives it whether it will prove voidable, so his tendency will be to grab it and hope, and perhaps even to manipulate his relationship with the debtor to delay the inevitable bankruptcy . . . .").

2.8.4 Conclusion

There is no question that the clawback preference laws siphon back creditor dollars to the bankruptcy estate.[53] There is reason to doubt, though, that much of the clawed-back cash goes to the supposed beneficiaries, i.e., unsecured creditors.

---

53. Hall, *supra* note 9, at 51-52 (explaining that because creditor's intent is no longer relevant, and absent a § 547(c) exception, "the trustee may recover all of the debtor's property preferentially transferred within ninety days of bankruptcy"); *see also id.* at 80 (stating that courts "broadly constru[e] the preferential transfer provisions, while placing restrictions on the availability of statutory exceptions and setoff").

CHAPTER 3

What Are My Defenses?

Winston Churchill said about democracy that it's the worst system except for all the others.[54] The general attitude among lawmakers and scholarly folks is that the same is correct about the preference laws. There are a lot of problems with them, but they're the best we can do, and they're better than nothing.[55]

I happen to think the laws do more harm than good.

Whether the preference laws are worth it or not, Congress did mitigate their impact by arming creditors with many effective defenses.[56]

In addition to these statutory defenses, sympathetic judges have permitted "equitable" arguments that are nowhere in the Bankruptcy Code but

---

54. Winston Churchill, Address Before the House of Commons (Nov. 11, 1947), in *Winston S Churchill: His Complete Speeches 1897-1963*, at 7566 (Robert Rhodes James ed., 1974) (famously saying that "democracy is the worst form of Government except for all those other forms that have been tried from time to time").

55. Tabb, *supra* note 9, at 409 (citing Countryman, *supra* note 37, at 748) (noting that "without a preference recapture law, the bankruptcy distributional scheme could be subverted by transfers made on the eve of bankruptcy. Little would be left for those creditors who were not fortunate or diligent enough to obtain a prebankruptcy preference."); *see also* Brook E. Gotberg, *Conflicting Preferences in Business Bankruptcy: The Need for Different Rules in Different Chapters*, 100 Iowa L. Rev. 51, 53 (2014) ("Preferential transfer law in bankruptcy has long been the subject of significant controversy.").

56. 11 U.S.C. § 547(c); *see also* Hall, supra note 9, at 67-68 ("Section 547(c) precludes the trustee from avoiding certain preferential transfers despite proof of Section 547(b)'s requirements. This section is designed to preserve transactions which are considered essential to commercial practices or which may afford debtors an opportunity to keep their businesses afloat in the face of bankruptcy.").

are supported by policy and fairness.[57]

In this section, I will describe both the statutory and equitable defenses to a preference clawback lawsuit.

3.1   Defending Your Case

There are two basic types of defenses:

- Plead "not guilty"—argue that the trustee failed to prove that you got a preferential transfer.

- Plead "guilty with an explanation"—admit you received a preference but raise defenses.[58]

You can try one of these or both.

The trustee has a "laundry list" of facts[59] that he must prove to establish that you received a preference. If you convince the judge that the trustee failed to properly allege these facts or cannot prove these facts, the judge might dismiss the case.[60]

The trustee's laundry list:[61]

- The payment came from the property of the debtor.[62]

- The payment was made to you, and you are a creditor.[63]

---

57. Kevin M. Baum, Note: *Apparently, "No Good Deed Goes Unpunished"*: *The Earmarking Doctrine, Equitable Subrogation, and Inquiry Notice Are Necessary Protections When Refinancing Consumer Mortgages in an Uncertain Credit Market,** Chase Manhattan Mortgage Corp. v. Shapiro (In re Lee), *530 F.3d 458, 475 (6th Cir. 2008) (Merritt, J., dissenting),"* 83 St. John's L. Rev. 1361, 1374 (2009) (noting that despite the defenses provided in § 547(c), there are "common law defenses" that the defendant-creditor can assert: "the 'earmarking doctrine,' 'equitable subrogation,' and 'inquiry notice.'").

58. There is no defense called "guilty with an explanation" in the bankruptcy code. I made this phrase up because I think it describes the legal philosophy behind these defenses.

59. *See supra* note 28 and accompanying text.

60. Hall, *supra* note 9, at 68 (citing H.R. Rep. No. 595, 95th Cong., 1st Sess. n.22, at 177, 373-74 (1977)) ("Success in one or more of Section 547(c)'s exception provisions will protect the transfer to the extent allowed by those exceptions.").

61. This is my simplified summary of the trustee's burden of proof, which is found in total in 11 U.S.C. § 547(b).

62. Gotberg, *supra* note 57, at 66 ("The elements of an avoidable preference, as defined by the Bankruptcy Code, require a transfer of the debtor's property to a creditor, on account of a previous debt, made during the 90 days prior to the filing of the bankruptcy petition, such that the creditor received more than it would have under a bankruptcy liquidation and distribution of the debtor's assets.").

63. *Id.*

- The payment was made to pay an antecedent debt.[64]

- The debtor is insolvent (there is a presumption that this is the case, but it is rebuttable).[65]

- You received the money within 90 days before the bankruptcy case was filed.[66]

- You would have received less if the case had been a Chapter 7 bankruptcy case at the time you were paid.[67]

3.2   The Trustee Didn't Prove His Case!

I will describe ways to attack the trustee's above-described laundry list using our Moe, Larry, and Curly hypothetical. (As a reminder, Moe borrows $10,000 each from Larry and Curly, repays Curly $10,000, pays Larry nothing, and files for bankruptcy.). In summary, Curly's primary defense arguments are:

- I got the payment, but it was not the debtor's property.

- I got the payment, but I wasn't a "creditor," and the payment was not payment of antecedent debt.

- I got the payment, but the debtor had enough money to pay everybody in full, so there is no need for a clawback—I didn't get an advantage over other creditors.

- I got the payment, but I would've been paid 100% anyway during a Chapter 7 bankruptcy.

- I didn't get the payment during the preference period.

---

64. *Id.*

65. *Id.* at 66-67 (stating that the Bankruptcy Code "establishes a rebuttable presumption for insolvency during the 90-day preference period"); *see also* 11 U.S.C. § 547(f).

66. Gotberg, *supra* note 57, at 66 (citing 11 U.S.C. § 547(b)(4) (requiring that for a transfer to be preferential it must have been made "within the 90 days before the date of the filing or between 90 days and one year prior to the filing, if the creditor is an insider")).

67. *Id.* (citing 11 U.S.C. 547(b)(5) (requiring that for a transfer to be preferential the transfer "'enables [a preferred creditor] to receive more than such creditor would receive if the transfer had not been made and the estate distributed according to the rules of a Chapter 7 liquidation")).

3.2.1   I Got the Payment, but It Was Not the Debtor's Money

If Moe paid Curly with money held in trust for Curly, the clawback case against Curly might fail. Larry could not complain about this situation since Moe is just transferring Curly's property to Curly. Usually, the payment you get is the debtor's property, but here are some examples of situations where this defense may apply.

Since, in the below examples, the money did not belong to the debtor, *it would never have been available to other unsecured creditors.* Since other unsecured creditors would not have received any part of these funds, it's not unfair that the defendant got paid in full.

3.2.1.1   Statutory Trust

The debtor is a general contractor who pays a subcontractor from funds that he holds in trust for the subcontractor under state law. The subcontractor may defeat a clawback.

3.2.1.2   Constructive Trust

The debtor is a payment processor and paid the IRS from funds that were held in trust for the IRS to pay taxes. The IRS may defeat a clawback.

3.2.1.3   Actual trust

The debtor is a law firm that paid its client money it was holding in trust for the client. The client/defendant[68] might argue successfully that the funds never "belonged" to the debtor and never passed into the bankruptcy estate because they were trust funds held for the client.

3.2.1.4   Stolen Money

A debtor who ran a Ponzi scheme pays a landlord. The landlord might argue successfully that the money paid did not belong to the debtor but rather was stolen money that belonged to "investors."

---

68. A defendant is an "individual (or business) against whom a lawsuit is filed." United States Courts, *Bankruptcy Basics Glossary*, http://www.uscourts.gov/educational-resources/educational-activities/bankruptcy-basics-glossary. In this book, the defendant is the creditor who is alleged to have made a preferential payment that should be clawed back.

3.2.1.5 The Earmarking Defense

The earmarking defense is an equitable defense that is not spelled out in the Bankruptcy Code.[69] Many judges agreed with the argument on fairness grounds, and it became ensconced in a line of cases that other judges could follow[70] (without too much fear of being reversed at the district court level).

The earmarking defense works like this:

- A new lender provides cash to the debtor with the specific written requirement that the funds can only be used to pay a particular creditor.[71]

- These new funds are then used by the debtor to pay that particular creditor.[72]

- The net result is that a new creditor has been substituted for an old creditor.[73] In other words, the debtor still owes the same amount of money, and the debtor's property has not been depleted.

The rationale for the defense is that the payment is not unfair to other creditors because the debtor just switched creditors, with the net effect of no diminution of the debtor's assets.[74]

---

69. David Gray Carlson & William H. Widen, *The Earmarking Defense to Voidable Preference Liability: A Reconceptualization,* 73 Am. Bankr. L.J. 591, 591 (1999) ("Earmarking is said to be an extra-statutory, judge-created exception to § 547(b) liability." (citing McCuskey v. National Bank of Waterloo (*In re* Bohlen Enterprises, Ltd.), 859 F.2d 561, 565 (8th Cir. 1988))); *see also* Hansen v. MacDonald Meat Co. (*In re* Kemp Pacific Fisheries, Inc.), 16 F.3d 313, 316 n.2 (9th Cir. 1994) (calling earmarking "a creature of equity").

70. *See* National Bank of Newport v. National Herkimer Cty. Bank of Little Falls, 225 U.S. 178, 32 S. Ct. 633, 56 L. Ed. 1042 (1912) (holding that a new creditor's payment to an old creditor did not constitute a voidable transfer of the debtor's property); *see also* First Nat'l Bank of Danville, Ill. v. Phalen, 62 F.2d 21 (7th Cir. 1932) (holding that a check made out to a debtor with instructions to endorse the check to the old creditor constitutes earmarking); Grubb v. General Contract Purchase Corp., 94 F.2d 70 (2d Cir. 1938) (finding that earmarking exists where the new lender himself directly pays the old creditor); Western Tie and Timber Co. v. Brown, 196 U.S. 502 (1905); New York Cty. Nat'l Bank v. Massey, 192 U.S. 138 (1901).

71. 5-547 *Collier on Bankruptcy* 547.03[2][a] (16th ed. 2016) ("A widely held exception to section 547 holds that when a third person makes a loan to a debtor specifically to enable that debtor to satisfy the claim of a designated creditor, the proceeds never become part of the debtor's assets, and therefore no preference is created.").

72. *Id.* (stating that the funds are given to the debtor by the new creditor "with the understanding that they will be paid to the creditor in satisfaction of the creditor's claim").

73. *Id.* (noting that under the earmarking doctrine "[o]ne creditor has been substituted for another").

74. *Id.* (opining that there is no unfairness because "the property 'transferred' in such a situation was never property of the debtor and so the transfer did not disadvantage other creditors").

The critical element is whether the debtor had control over the funds that were paid to it by the new creditor or whether the new creditor structured the loan so that the debtor had no control over the money.[75]

For example, if the new creditor paid the money directly to the old creditor, then the debtor had no control over the money. If the new creditor paid the money to the debtor, then the debtor theoretically could have paid whoever it wanted to pay, and the defense might not apply.[76]

The key, again, is the absence of circumstantial evidence pointing to the debtor's intention to favor the old creditor over all its other creditors.[77] If the debtor had no control over the funds, then it *could not have demonstrated an intent* to prefer a particular creditor.[78] On the other hand, if the debtor had control of the funds for some time, it could have *chosen* to prefer the old creditor, and might have had a preferential intent.[79] (A debtor's intention is not relevant, of course, except that it is.)

3.2.1.6 The PACA or PASA Defense

If you shipped fresh produce or poultry to the debtor and got paid during the 90-day preference period, you might nevertheless be immune from a preference clawback lawsuit.[80] Two federal statutes, the Perishable Agricultural Commodities Act (PACA) and the Packers and Stockyards Act (PASA), create a trust for vendors.[81]

---

75. *Id.* ("The 'key' to the resolution of whether a preferential occurred 'centers on whether [the debtor] had any control of the [subsidiary's] collateral during the repayment of [the debtor's] loan when the preference allegedly occurred." (quoting Coral Petroleum, Inc. v. Banque Paribas-London, 797 F.2d 1351,1358 (5th Cir. 1986))).

76. Coral Petroleum, Inc. v. Banque Paribas-London, 797 F.2d 1351, 1361 (5th Cir. 1986) ("Where the debtor physically receives control of the funds, there can still be an 'earmark' . . . but the debtor's lack of dispositive control must be proven.").

77. *Id.* at 1362 (noting that "the crucial fact" is whether "[the debtor] control[led] the money to the extent that it became property of its estate").

78. *Id.* ("[The creditor's] control of the use of [the subsidiary's] collateral would not constitute a preference because to look to the identity of the actual earmarker is to lose sight of the fact that whoever it was, it was not [the debtor].").

79. Adams v. Anderson (*In re* Superior Stamp & Coin Co., Inc.), 223 F.3d 1004, 1009, 44 C.B.C. 2d 1382 (9th Cir. 2000) ("[T]he proper inquiry is not whether the funds entered the debtor's account, but whether the debtor had the right to disburse the funds to whomever it wished, or whether [the] disbursement was limited to a particular old creditor or creditors under the agreement with the new creditor.").

80. *In re* Fresh Approach, Inc., 51 B.R. 412 (Bankr. N.D. Tex. 1985) (finding that a produce supplier's interest in a Perishable Agricultural Commodities Act trust is not a preference subject to avoidance).

81. *See* Perishable Agricultural Commodities Act, 7 U.S.C. § 499(a); Packers and Stockyards Act, 1921, 7 U.S.C. §§ 181-

If you ship the type of produce or meat listed in the statutes (and follow the rules regarding notice and other matters), *payments* for those products are trust funds.[82]

If payments are trust funds, then they are not the debtor's property.[83] Since the debtor can only claw back money that belonged to it, these funds cannot be clawed back.[84]

The main hurdle with this defense is proving that these statutes cover the product that you delivered. (For example, is a payment for dried berries protected? You will need to look at the PACA statute to find out.)[85]

The second challenge is proving that you followed the procedures the statutes require.[86] Under PACA the vendor must have provided written notice that the product falls under the PACA.[87] A lot of vendors shrewdly put this notice in all their invoices. If written notice was not provided, the vendor loses all protection.[88]

3.2.1.7 The Constructive Trust Defense

If the debtor received funds from you because of a mistake on your part and the debtor returned that money to you during the preference period, the trustee might be unable to later sue you successfully for a preference. The argument is that the debtor never had any legal or equitable interest in the money and had essentially converted it. The debtor was just holding the money in constructive trust for you, and you were

---

231.

82. East Coast Potato Distributors v. Grant (*In re* Super Spud, Inc.), 77 B.R. 930 (Bankr. M.D. Fla. 1987) (finding that the property held by the bankrupt in trust belongs to the trust beneficiary and never became part of the bankruptcy estate).

83. *Id.*

84. Mitsui Mfrs. Bank v. Unicom Computer Corp. (*In re* Unicom Computer Corp.), 13 F.3d 321 (9th Cir. 1994) (finding that something held in trust by debtor for another is neither property of bankruptcy estate nor property of debtor for purposes of voiding preferential payments).

85. *In re Fresh Approach*, 51 B.R. at 418-19 (stating that PACA "allow[s] for the creation of a trust for the benefit of unpaid produce creditors . . . so long as such beneficiaries perfect their interests pursuant to the statute or its implementing regulations").

86. *Id.*

87. 7 U.S.C. § 499(c)(3) ("The unpaid supplier, seller, or agent shall lose the benefits of such trust unless such person has given written notice of intent to preserve the benefits of the trust to the commission merchant, dealer, or broker . . . .").

88. *Id.*

not a creditor of the debtor.[89] Constructive trust issues are matters of state law that the bankruptcy court must apply so results may differ in different jurisdictions.

3.2.2 I Got the Payment, but I Wasn't a "Creditor," and the Payment Was Not Payment of an Antecedent Debt

In Curly's situation, my hypothetical states that Curly was a creditor. To remove any doubt, go to the definition section of the Bankruptcy Code and look up "creditor."[90] The Bankruptcy Code defines a creditor as someone with a right to payment. Curly had a right to payment, so he was a creditor.

Moe also paid Curly an "antecedent" debt. "Antecedent" is not defined in the Bankruptcy Code, so we are forced to assume a common sense meaning (always a dangerous assumption in the bankruptcy world). A debt was created when Moe began owing money to Curly. Later, Moe paid Curly. The debt "was antecedent to" (existed before) its payment. Therefore, the payment was payment of an antecedent debt.

Here are some examples where the payment might not be payment of an antecedent debt.

- The payment was a prepayment.

  - You're a software designer. Your contract stipulated that the client will pay you in advance. The client did indeed pay you before you handed over your work product. You argue that this payment was a prepayment and not payment of an "antecedent debt."[91]

---

89. Claybrook v. Consolidated Foods, Inc. (*In re* Bake-Line Grp., LLC), 359 B.R. 566, 571 (Bankr. D. Del. 2007) ("'A constructive trust is imposed to prevent unjust enrichment by imposing a duty on the person receiving the benefit to convey the property back to the person from which it was received.'" (quoting Martin v. Heinold Commodities, 643 N.E.2d 734, 745 (1994))); *id.* ("'The sole duty of the constructive trustee is to transfer title and possession of the wrongfully acquired property to the beneficiary.'" (quoting Suttles v. Vogel, 533 N.E.2d 901, 904 (1988))).

90. 11 U.S.C § 101(10) ("(**10**) The term "creditor" means— (**A**) entity that has a claim against the debtor that arose at the time of or before the order for relief concerning the debtor . . . ." ("(**5**) The term 'claim' means— (**A**) right to payment, whether or not such right is reduced to judgment, liquidated, unliquidated, fixed, contingent, matured, unmatured, disputed, undisputed, legal, equitable, secured, or unsecured . . . .").

91. *See In re* Middendorf, 381 B.R. 774, 778-79 (Bankr. D. Kan. 2008) (finding that a debtor's payment to the IRS was a pre-payment and therefore did not constitute a preference because the payment was not made on an antecedent debt).

- The debtor gave you a gift.

  - If the debtor gave you money as a gift or bonus, you could argue that this is not payment of an antecedent debt.[92]

- You are a "conduit."[93]

  - You're the agent for a cruise line. The cruise line pays you to stock up on provisions for a cruise. You use the money to pay suppliers. You can argue that the payment was not payment of an antecedent debt--you were merely a conduit of the money.

- Escrow accounts.[94]

  - You are an attorney. A company wires your law firm $10,000 for you to put in an escrow account for your client. Within 90 days of wiring you these funds, the company files for bankruptcy. A trustee sues you to recover the money as a preferential transfer. The company did not owe your law firm any money. Therefore, it was arguably not paying *you* an antecedent debt.

3.2.3 The Conduit Defense

The conduit defense gets its own subsection since it can be a robust defense. As in the cruise line example above, the conduit defense applies to situations where the debtor paid one entity, but that entity primarily acted as a pass-through and transferred the funds to another entity, where the monies rested.[95] The argument is that you never received the debtor's

---

92. Tidwell v. Galbreath (*In re* Galbreath), 207 B.R. 309 (Bankr. M.D. Ga. 1997) (finding that a gift is not in payment of an antecedent debt which constitutes an avoidable preference under Section 547).

93. Bonded Fin. Servs., Inc. v. European Am. Bank, 838 F.2d 890 (7th Cir. 1988) (finding that a bank who received a payment from a debtor, and then passed along the payment to a third party, is a "mere conduit" because it was not the "beneficial transferee").

94. Burch v. Bonded Adjusters, Inc. (*In re* Estates of Pelc), 34 B.R. 823 (Bankr. D. Or. 1983) (finding no voidable preference and no transfer of property of the debtors where there is a distribution of an installment to judgment creditors pursuant to escrow instructions); *see also* Gropper v. Unitrac, S.A. (*In re* Fabric Buys of Jericho, Inc.), 33 B.R. 334 (Bankr. S.D.N.Y. 1983) (finding that a law firm maintaining an escrow account for a transferee acted as a mere conduit and, therefore, was not the initial transferee).

95. 5-550 *Collier on Bankruptcy* 550.02[4][a] (16th ed. 2016) (stating that "many courts have found that a party acting merely as a conduit who facilitates the transfer from the debtor to a third party is not a 'transferee' and, therefore, not the initial transferee" in which case the transfer could be avoided); *see also* First Nat'l Bank of Barnesville v. Rafoth (*In re* Baker & Getty Fin. Servs., Inc.), 974 F.2d 712, 721-22, 27 C.B.C. 2d 1112 (6th Cir. 1992) (finding that bank was the initial transferee when it had an individual deposit proceeds of a sale of the debtor's assets in the individual's account until the

payment in the sense of taking title to the money and you are not a creditor. It is a legal fiction that is not found explicitly in the Bankruptcy Code. Rather, it is a judge-created doctrine rooted in fairness. Examples of conduit situations follow:

- An end user pays a general contractor funds it directs to be paid to a subcontractor.

- A business wires money to an advertising agency to be used to buy television advertising time.

Most courts require that the funds be paid to the conduit *first* and that the conduit *then* use those funds to pay the debtor's creditors.

If the "conduit" *advances* money to pay creditors and then looks back to be reimbursed by the debtor, it may lose conduit status. The theory is that, in those circumstances, advancing the money created an antecedent debt, which the debtor later paid. So the payment paid an antecedent debt, and the defense will not apply.

If the recipient of the funds pays others *after* receiving the funds, then *at the time of receiving the funds* he was not a creditor since he was not owed any money.

3.2.4 The Debtor Was Able to Pay Everybody 100 Cents on the Dollar When I Got Paid

If a debtor can pay everyone 100 cents on the dollar, then suing a creditor for a preference would make no sense.

The whole purpose is to right the wrong of a lucky creditor getting paid in *full* before the bankruptcy in situations where other creditors are later only being paid a *small percentage* of their claims. You cannot be a "preferred" creditor if *everybody* gets paid 100%.

In our situation, we said that Moe did not have enough assets to pay both Larry and Curly in full. Therefore, Moe was insolvent: his assets were worth less than his liabilities.

---

funds cleared; the funds were then applied against an obligation of the debtor to the bank).

However, it does not necessarily follow that because a company files for bankruptcy, its assets are worth less than its liabilities. Many debtors file because they don't have the cash flow to pay debts that are coming due.[96] In other words, they cannot liquidate their assets fast enough to pay current obligations and don't have enough income to pay current debts.

For example, maybe Moe didn't have the cash to pay Larry and Curly, but he did own a Ferrari worth more than his debts. To avoid selling his Ferrari at a fire sale, he filed for Chapter 11 bankruptcy. In Chapter 11 he could keep his car and pay his debts over time. Moe was solvent. The preference case against Curly would have to be dismissed since a trustee would eventually pay Larry a hundred cents on the dollar.

3.2.5   Contesting Insolvency

If a preference defendant has sufficient evidence that the debtor was solvent at the time of the transfer, she might consider challenging the "rebuttable presumption of insolvency."[97] The Bankruptcy Code's "presumption of insolvency" means that the trustee gets a preliminary free ride—the trustee doesn't need to prove insolvency. The debtor is presumed insolvent in the 90-day period before the bankruptcy. "Rebuttable" means that if you provide some evidence of solvency to the bankruptcy judge, the court might decide that the presumption is negated and require the trustee to prove insolvency.[98]

The main problem with contesting insolvency is that it's costly to litigate. First, you need to find the right evidence to successfully rebut the pre-

---

96. Burtch v. Opus, LLC (*In re* Opus East, LLC), 528 B.R. 30, 51 (Bankr. D. Del. 2015) (stating that insolvency can be "proven under the 'cash flow' test if at the time of a transfer, the debtor intended to incur or believed that it would incur debts beyond its ability to pay as such debts matured" (citing EBC I, Inc. v. Am. Online, Inc. (*In re* EBC I, Inc.), 380 B.R. 348 (Bankr. D. Del. 2008))).

97. H.R. REP. No. 595, 95th Cong., 1st Sess. 177-79 (1977) (stating that the presumption of insolvency can be rebutted by the transferee of the preference by presenting evidence to overcome the presumption); 5-547 *Collier on Bankruptcy* 547.12 (16th. ed. 2016) (stating that a creditor defending a preference action has to produce "some evidence" that the debtor was solvent at the time the transfer was made).

98. *See id.*

sumption.[99] Second, you will have to hire an expert.[100]

What follows is the kind of rigmarole Curly might have to endure to contest insolvency in the above hypothetical:

- Curly would have to show the court that the Ferrari was worth at least $20,000.

- He would have to have the car formally appraised at his expense.

- He might want to obtain from some reliable source comparisons of car valuations.

- The trustee would probably fight Curly by objecting to Curly's evidence.

- Curly would have to hire an expert, who might charge more than the $10,000 Curly is owed.

- The trustee would hire his own expert to contradict Curly's expert.

- Curly would tear out his hair (if he had any).

In the realm of corporate bankruptcy, proving solvency can be complicated, expensive, and uncertain.[101] You need an expert to go over the debtor's books and records and decide whether the debtor was insolvent.[102] Sometimes assets are valued for less than they should be. Sometimes liabilities are exaggerated.

The costs involved in contesting insolvency add up fast:

---

99. Lawson v. Ford Motor Co. (*In re* Roblin Indus., Inc.), 78 F.3d 30, 35 (2nd Cir. 1996) (stating that "[i]nsolvency is a question of fact" and bankruptcy courts have broad discretion when considering evidence of whether an entity is solvent or insolvent (citing Klein v. Tabatchnick, 610 F.2d 1043, 1048 (2d Cir. 1979))).

100. *See* Brandt v. Samuel, Son & Co., Ltd. (*In re* Longview Aluminum, L.L.C.), Case No. 03 B 12184, 2005 Bankr. LEXIS 1312, at *17 (Bankr. N.D. Ill. 2005) ("It is generally accepted that whenever possible, a determination of insolvency should be based on seasonable appraisals or expert testimony."); *see also* Brothers Gourmet Coffees, Inc. v. Armenia Coffee Corp. (*In re* Brothers Gourmet Coffees, Inc.), 271 B.R. 456 (Bankr. D. Del. 2002) (finding that defendant successfully rebutted debtor's presumption of insolvency by presenting expert testimony, which created a material issue of fact and defeated summary judgment).

101. Stan Bernstein, Susan H. Seabury, & Jack F. Williams, *Squaring Bankruptcy Valuation Practice with Daubert Demands*, 16 Am. Bankr. Inst. L. Rev. 161, 162 (2008) (describing the complicated nature of expert testimony in bankruptcy cases and opining that "[a]ttorneys, financial advisers, turnaround managers, and experts on the valuation of businesses are becoming more sophisticated in the developing sub-discipline of valuing distressed businesses").

102. *Id.*

- the hourly charge by an expert to do a preliminary analysis

- the cost of paying an expert to produce a written report

- the cost of paying an expert to appear for depositions, including travel time, hotels, and other expenses

- the cost of paying an expert to appear in court, including travel time, hotels, and other expenses

- the cost of paying an expert to draft a supplemental report rebutting the plaintiff's[103] expert report

Two critical points to remember:

- First, the trustee only has a rebuttable presumption of insolvency. If you present enough evidence of solvency, the presumption might be removed, and the trustee will have the burden of proving solvency.[104]

- Second, courts define insolvency in a couple of ways.[105]

  o One definition is called "balance sheet insolvency." This insolvency analysis is exactly what it sounds like.[106] The court analyzes the balance sheet to determine whether liabilities exceed assets based on the immediate forced liquidation of the assets (a "fire sale").[107]

  o The second way of determining insolvency is to weigh the "going concern value" as an additional asset.[108] In other words, this defi-

---

103. A plaintiff is a "person or business that files a formal complaint with the court." United States Courts, *Bankruptcy Basics Glossary*, http://www.uscourts.gov/educational-resources/educational-activities/bankruptcy-basics-glossary.

104. 5-547 *Collier on Bankruptcy* 547.12 (16th ed. 2016) (stating that a creditor defending a preference action has to produce "some evidence" that the debtor was solvent at the time the transfer was made).

105. *See id.*

106. Bruce R. Kraus, Note, *Preferential Transfers and the Value of the Insolvent Firm*, 87 Yale L.J. 1449, 1460-61 (1978) (stating that "insolvency for preference purposes is measured under a balance sheet test").

107. Lawrence Ponoroff, *Evil Intentions and An Irresolute Endorsement for Scientific Rationalism: Bankruptcy Preferences One More Time*, 1993 Wis. L. Rev. 1439 (1993) (citing Bayless Manning & James J. Hanks, Jr., *Legal Capital* 63-64 (3d. ed. 1990) (noting that balance sheet insolvency emphasizes net tangible worth on liquidation of the enterprise)).

108. Wolkowitz v. American Research Corp. (*In re DAK Industries, Inc.*), 170 F.3d 1197, 1199-1200 (9th Cir. 1999) (stating that "[a] 'fair valuation' of a debtor's assets must begin with a determination of whether a debtor is 'a going concern'"); *see also* Trans World Airlines, Inc. v. Travellers Int'l AG. (*In re Trans World Airlines, Inc.*), 180 B.R. 389, 404 (Bankr. D. Del. 1994) (noting that both parties agreed that "the valuation should be done on a 'going concern' basis); Lids Corp. v. Marathon Inv. Partners, L.P. (*In re Lids Corp.*), 281 B.R. 535, 541 (Bankr. D. Del. 2002) ("A 'going concern'

nition values the company as a business, not just a list of unused buildings or machinery.[109] Again, this is an expensive analysis that is typically performed by distressed valuation experts.[110]

3.2.6 I Was Not Paid during the Preference Period

We assumed in our example that Moe paid Curly a week before Moe filed for bankruptcy.

Here is an example of arguing that you were *not* paid during the preference period.

- Let's say you received a check but never deposited it. The date a check clears is one of the factors a court considers when determining when a transfer was made.[111] So, if you received the check before the 90-day period starts and it clears during the 90-day period, you were paid in the 90-day period.[112] On the other hand, if you received the check during the 90-day period but did not deposit it, you can argue that there was no transfer during the preference period under the Bankruptcy Code.[113]

---

is a commercial enterprise actively engaging in business with the expectation of indefinite continuance.").

109. Bernstein, Seabury, & Williams, *supra* note 104, at 172 (stating that "to determine the value of a debtor at any given point in time, an expert should first determine . . . the fair market value of the debtor as a going concern"); *see also In re Lids Corp.*, 281 B.R. at 541 ("As long as liquidation in bankruptcy is not clearly imminent on the Valuation Date, the company must be valued as a going concern.").

110. *Id.* (describing generally how experts should determine "going concern").

111. Hall, *supra* note 9, at 61 ("Authority is split on when a transfer by check occurs.").

112. Hall, *supra* note 9, at 61-62 (explaining that one view "considers a check to be transferred upon delivery. This approach deems a check to be a cash equivalent which is exchanged contemporaneously between parties. Delivery of the check suspends the debtor's obligation, whereas acceptance of the check suspends the creditor's right to sue on that obligation until the check is presented for payment." (citing *In re* Sider Ventures & Servs. Corp., 33 B.R. 708 (Bankr. S.D.N.Y. 1983))).

113. *Id.* at 61 ("A check *per se* does not grant a creditor an interest in the debtor's funds; therefore, the transfer remains ineffective until the bank issues payment."); *see generally In re* Bob Grissett Golf Shoppes, Inc., 34 B.R. 320 (Bankr. E.D. Va. (1983); *In re* Georgia Steel, Inc., 38 B.R. 829 (Bankr. M.D. Ga. 1984); *see also In re* Morton Shoe Companies, Inc., 36 Bankr. 320, 9 B.C.D. 654 (Bankr. D. Mass. 1983).

3.2.7 I Would've Been Paid 100 Cents on the Dollar Anyway in a Hypothetical Chapter 7 Bankruptcy Even if the Company Were Insolvent

This element presents a hypothetical: If you had *not* been paid *and* this case had been a Chapter 7 liquidation case, would you have been paid *less* in the bankruptcy than the amount you actually received?

This section primarily protects fully secured creditors.

If collateral secured your debt, you would have been paid in full in a hypothetical Chapter 7 bankruptcy case whether the debtor was insolvent or not. Secured creditors are paid to the extent they are secured by collateral. An intervening bankruptcy makes no difference.

This section makes perfect sense. A secured creditor getting paid in full during the preference period receives no advantage since it would've been paid in full anyway during the bankruptcy. A *secured* creditor gets paid in full with money that would *never* have been available to *unsecured* creditors.

Fully secured creditors generally get paid 100 cents on the dollar during the bankruptcy.[114] Here are some examples of how you can use this defense:

- Be a mortgage lender. These lenders have liens against the debtor's property that collateralize their debt and exempt it from bankruptcy.[115] After the bankruptcy, you will still get paid up to 100 cents on the dollar because bankruptcy does not affect your collateral.[116] If you have a lien on the debtor's house, even if the trustee sells the house, you will be paid up to the value of the lien.

- Have a mechanic's lien against the debtor's property.[117] The same

---

114. Jackson, *supra* note 16, at 769 (noting that it is a principle in bankruptcy that "secured creditors are entitled to be paid in full first").

115. *See* H.R. Rep. No. 595, 95th Cong., 1st Sess. 382 (1977) (stating that Congress, in creating the Bankruptcy Code, wanted to give courts "the authority to ensure that collateral or its proceeds is returned to the proper secured creditor").

116. *Id.*

117. William M. Hensley, *Worlds in Collision: Mechanic's Liens and Federal Bankruptcy Schemes Confront Each Other and How the Courts Reconcile the Conflict*, 31 Whittier L. Rev. 621, 662 (2010) ("Where a mechanic's lien has actually been recorded against a debtor's property, a payment to release this lien will likely not be avoidable as a preference . . . .").

principle applies. Any valid mechanic's lien-secured creditor will generally get paid in full.[118] That's why you don't see secured creditors complaining about the preference laws. They are exempt.[119] The only caveat is that you get paid to the extent of the equity in the property covered by the lien and no more. (The wrinkles involved in payments to secured creditors are beyond the scope of this book.)

- Have a surety.[120] A surety is someone other than the debtor who guaranteed the debtor's obligations to you. For example, if there existed a construction bond that secured payment to you as a subcontractor even if the general contractor ended up not paying you, the construction bond company could be characterized as a surety. The argument is that you would've been paid in full by the surety in a hypothetical Chapter 7 bankruptcy.[121]

3.2.8   The Hypothetical Lien Defense[122]

This argument is that a creditor that *could* have filed a lien, but did not only because it was paid, should be treated as if it had filed a lien if sued for a clawback.

The hypothetical lien defense challenges the trustee's proof that a creditor was paid more in the preference period[123] than he would have been

---

118. Schwinn Plan Comm. v. Transamerica Ins. Fin. Corp. (*In re* Schwinn Bicycle Co.), 200 B.R. 980, 991 (Bankr. N.D. Ill. 1996) (mentioning that it is a rule in bankruptcy that "fully secured creditors cannot be preferenced[;] . . . transfers to a fully secured creditor are exempt from the avoidance provisions of the Bankruptcy Code") (citing Matter of Prescott, 805 F.2d 719, 726 (7th Cir. 1986)).

119. *Id.*

120. *See* 11 U.S.C. § 547(d).

121. Lubman v. C.A. Guard Masonry Contr., Inc. (*In re* Gem Constr. Corp. of Va.), 262 B.R. 638 (Bankr. E.D. Va. 2000) (citing Pearlman v. Reliance Ins. Co., 371 U.S. 132, 140-41, 83 S. Ct. 232, 9 L. Ed. 2d 190 (1962) (holding that "a construction contract surety who completes a payment for a defaulting contractor obtains a common-law equitable right of subrogation to contract proceeds, which is superior to the interests of the bankruptcy estate")); *see also* O'Rourke v. Coral Constr., Inc. (*In re* E.R. Fegert, Inc.), 88 B.R. 258, 260 (B.A.P. 9th Cir. 1988) (holding that new value is given where there are sufficient identifiable contract proceeds to satisfy the surety's equitable lien).

122. *See* 11 U.S.C. § 547(b) ("Except as provided in subsections (c) and (i) of this section, the trustee may avoid any transfer of an interest of the debtor in property— . . . (5) that enables such creditor to receive more than such creditor would receive if—(A) the case were a case under chapter 7 of this title; (B) the transfer had not been made; and (C) such creditor received payment of such debt to the extent provided by the provisions of this title.")

123. *See* 11 U.S.C. § 547(b)(5)(A).

paid in a hypothetical Chapter 7 case.[124]

As seen above, section 547(b)(5) of the Bankruptcy Code presents a hypothetical situation. It asks whether the creditor would have been paid less had the creditor *not* been paid and there had been a Chapter 7 bankruptcy filing. The so-called "hypothetical lien defense" takes the hypothetical presented in that Code section and stretches it out.

The argument is that if we are proposing a hypothetical, then we also must assume that the creditor would have acted rationally in that hypothetical situation.

If a rational creditor hypothetically had not been paid, he would have hypothetically filed a lien. If he had filed a hypothetical lien, then in the hypothetical Chapter 7 bankruptcy a trustee would have paid him in full.

The lawyer who invented this argument should get a (hypothetical) trophy. Judges bought the argument because they wanted to right the wrong of the following situation:

- First, the debtor pays a creditor.

- Second, if the debtor had not paid that creditor, the creditor would have been entitled to a lien.

- Third, the creditor does not assert a lien. The debtor paid so there was no need for a lien.

- Fourth, a trustee sues the creditor to get the money back as a preference.

- Fifth, the creditor, having no lien, is not secured, and there is no defense.

- Sixth, the creditor, tearing his hair out, argues that if he had known the money would later be clawed back, he would have filed a lien!

---

124. *Id.*; *see* also Zachman Homes, Inc. v. Oredson (*In re* Zachman Homes, Inc.), 40 B.R. 171, 173 (Bankr. D. Minn. 1984) ("The (b)(5) language is directed at transfers which diminish the estate available for distribution upon a Chapter 7 liquidation. Any transfer which diminishes or depletes the bankrupt's estate may be seen as a transfer which enables a creditor to receive more than other creditors of equal status and therefore is a preferential transfer.").

It seems highly unfair to trick a creditor into giving up his lien by paying him and then later clawing back the money.

The hypothetical lien defense says that if you had the right to assert a lien and make yourself a secured creditor if you were not paid, then the court should prevent a trustee from later clawing back the money.[125]

3.2.8.1 Problems That Can Come Up with This Defense

The trustee may argue that a hypothetical lien could render a creditor hypothetically secure only if hypothetically there had been enough equity in the debtor's property to support the full amount of the lien.

For example, the debtor pays you for construction work at one of the debtor's retail stores in a shopping mall. A Trustee sues you when the debtor goes bankrupt.. Your defense: if you had not been paid you would've put a mechanic's lien on the real estate on which the store was located. The trustee points out that the debtor leased the premises. The trustee argues that you could not have had a lien on the *debtor's* property since you did not work on the debtor's property—you worked on property that the debtor *leased*. There is a counter-argument, but that's beyond the scope of this handbook.

---

125. *See* John Deere Indus. Equip. Co. v. Southern Equip Sales Co., Inc. (*In re* Southern Equip. Sales Co., Inc.), 24 B.R. 788 (Bankr. D. N.J. 1982) (holding that transfer of funds to secured party made pursuant to agreement within 90-day preferential period does not create voidable preference under 11 USCS § 547(b)(5) where execution of agreement does not enable secured creditor to receive more than it would have if case were under Chapter 7 and agreement had not been made).

3.2.8.2 The Reclamation Defense[126]

The reclamation defense is based on the right of reclamation.[127] The right of reclamation gives you the theoretical right to "reclaim," or "take back," property you shipped to the debtor on the eve of a bankruptcy and for which you never got paid.[128]

The theory is that a company in the process of filing for bankruptcy ordered your product knowing it could not pay. Such conduct seems fraudulent.

You get a "right of reclamation" for unpaid-for goods shipped in the ordinary course in the 20-day period before the bankruptcy filing. (This section also provides for a reclamation right before this 20-day period, but various notices and other requirements are involved.)[129] This right of reclamation translates into an "administrative" claim against the estate.[130] Known as an "admin" claim by the cognoscenti, this is a special kind of claim that has priority over regular unsecured claims.[131]

---

126. *See* 11 U.S.C. § 546(c)(1):
   (1) Except as provided in subsection (d) of this section and in section 507(c), and subject to the prior rights of a holder of a security interest in such goods or the proceeds thereof, the rights and powers of the trustee under sections 544(a), 545, 547, and 549 are subject to the right of a seller of goods that has sold goods to the debtor, in the ordinary course of such seller's business, to reclaim such goods if the debtor has received such goods while insolvent, within 45 days before the date of the commencement of a case under this title, but such seller may not reclaim such goods unless such seller demands in writing reclamation of such goods—
   (A) not later than 45 days after the date of receipt of such goods by the debtor; or
   (B) not later than 20 days after the date of commencement of the case, if the 45-day period expires after the commencement of the case.

127. *See* 11 U.S.C. § 546(c).

128. Hitachi Denshi Amer., Ltd. v. Rozel Indus., Inc. (*In re* Rozel Indus., Inc.), 74 B.R. 643, 646 (Bankr. N.D. Ill. 1987) ("[T]his court finds that § 546(c) is the exclusive remedy for a seller seeking to reclaim goods from a debtor in bankruptcy. To obtain this remedy, the seller must meet the following requirements: (1) the seller must have a state statutory or common law right to reclaim the goods, (2) the seller must have sold the goods in the ordinary course of its business, (3) the debtor must have been insolvent when it received the goods, and (4) the seller must have made a written demand for the return of the goods within ten days after the debtor received the goods.").

129. *See* 11 U.S.C. § 546(c)(A) (providing that seller must demand in writing reclamation of goods "not later than 45 days after the date of receipt of such goods by the debtor;" *see also* 11 U.S.C. § 546(c)(1)(B) (providing that seller must demand in writing reclamation of goods "not later than 20 days after the date of commencement of the case, if the 45-day period expires after the commencement of the case").

130. *See* Lucas Aerospace, Inc. v. Continental Airlines, Inc. (*In re* Continental Airlines, Inc.), 171 B.R. 187, 189 (Bankr. D. Del. 1994) (noting that "[r]eclamation claims are granted priority status if allowed since they are considered administrative claims").

131. *In re* Toshiba Am., Inc. v. Video King of Ill., Inc. (*In re* Video King of Ill., Inc.), 100 B.R. 1008, 1016 (Bankr. N.D. Ill. 1989) ("Literally read, § 546(c) requires that the seller's full claim, not just the right to reclamation, be given administrative priority or secured by property of the estate where a seller is denied any rights of reclamation by the bankruptcy

The reclamation defense to a preference case stretches the hypothetical situation posed by 547(b)(5):

Posit as follows:

- You shipped product during the 20-day reclamation period.

- The debtor paid for that product.

- The trustee then sues to get back this payment as a preference.

- You invoke 547(b)(5) and say that if you *hadn't* been paid pre-petition, per the hypothetical, and were paid in a hypothetical Chapter 7 case, you would have been paid in full in the bankruptcy, so the payment to you is not unfair to other unsecured creditors.

- Why would you have been paid in full? If you had not been paid, you, being rational, would have filed a reclamation claim for the goods and received an administrative claim. Since admin claims get paid in full, you would have been paid in full.

Therefore, the trustee would be unable to prove his burden under 547 (b)(5)—you would *not* have been paid less in a hypothetical Chapter 7 bankruptcy.

. . . [so] the seller could have its entire $1,000,000 claim given administrative priority or secured by making a timely reclamation demand . . . .").

3.2.8.3 The Assumption Defense[132]

The assumption defense, like the reclamation defense, depends on the 547(b)(5) hypothetical.[133]

The Bankruptcy Code allows a company in bankruptcy to "assume" a defaulted contract if the debtor "cures" any default under the contract.[134] For example, a department store is leasing space in a shopping mall and has defaulted on the lease and is six months behind in rent when it files for bankruptcy. It can "assume," i.e., keep that breached lease in place, if it "cures," i.e., pays everything it owes under the lease (the six months' back rent).

Posit as follows:

- You are a landlord.

- You get paid three months' back rent during the preference period.

- The debtor "assumes" the lease in bankruptcy and cures all arrearages (it had owed six months' rent).

- The trustee sues you as a preferred creditor since you were paid the three months' back rent during the preference period.

- You argue that had you not been paid (per the 547(b)(5) hypothet-

---

132. *See* 11 U.S.C. § 365(c):

The trustee may not assume or assign any executory contract or unexpired lease of the debtor, whether or not such contract or lease prohibits or restricts assignment of rights or delegation of duties, if—

(1)

(A) applicable law excuses a party, other than the debtor, to such contract or lease from accepting performance from or rendering performance to an entity other than the debtor or the debtor in possession, whether or not such contract or lease prohibits or restricts assignment of rights or delegation of duties; and

(B) such party does not consent to such assumption or assignment; or

(2) such contract is a contract to make a loan, or extend other debt financing or financial accommodations, to or for the benefit of the debtor, or to issue a security of the debtor; or

(3) such lease is of nonresidential real property and has been terminated under applicable nonbankruptcy law prior to the order for relief.

133. *See* 11 U.S.C. § 365.

134. *Id.*; *see also* Weinman v. Allison Payment Sys., LLC (*In re* Centrix Fin., LLC), 434 B.R. 880, 886 (Bankr. D. Colo. 2010) ("[A] majority of courts . . . have recognized the Contract Assumption Defense as a complete bar to the trustee's avoidance powers."); *In re* Superior Toy & Mfg. Co., Inc., 78 F.3d 1169, 1174 (7th Cir. 1996) ("We believe Congress passed § 365 to insure that a contracting party is made whole before a court can force the party to continue performing with a bankrupt debtor. Permitting a preference suit after an assumption order would undermine that purpose.").

ical), you would have been paid in full anyway in a hypothetical bankruptcy.[135]

- The reason you would have been paid in full is that the debtor had assumed the lease and would, had you not been paid previously, paid you in full to cure the default and assume the lease.[136]

This is a challenging defense since it's going far out on the hypothetical limb.[137] But the defense reasoning is valid and unless the case law is settled against this argument in the Circuit where your case is located, it may be successful.

3.2.8.4 The Guarantor Defense

The guarantor defense is yet another 547(b)(5) defense. It works as follows. You're a subcontractor working for a general contractor. The owner/developer of the site bought insurance, which provided that if the general contractor didn't pay a subcontractor, the insurance company would pay the subcontractor. The general contractor goes bankrupt. A day before it files for bankruptcy, it pays you for work done on the site. The trustee sues you for a preference. You argue that under the 547(b)(5) hypothetical if you had not been paid by the general contractor, you would've been paid in full by the insurance company.[138]

The plaintiff would argue that the purpose of 547(b)(5) is to protect secured creditors. The argument is that full payment to secured creditors does not prejudice unsecured creditors because secured creditors would have been paid in full anyway in the bankruptcy. That rationale does not

---

135. *See* Alvarado v. Walsh (*In re* LCO Enterprises), 12 F.3d 938 (9th Cir. 1993); Kimmelman v. Port Auth. of N.Y. and N.J. (*In re* Kiwi Int'l Air Lines, Inc.), 344 F.3d 311 (3d Cir. 2003) (addressing the interplay of contract assumption and preference liability relying on a § 547(b)(5) analysis).

136. *In re Centrix Fin., LLC*, 434 B.R. at 887 ("Because § 365 requires the debtor to cure any default, it effectively places that creditor in a position similar to that of a fully secured creditor entitled to receive full payment on its claim. If a court calculates the hypothetical liquidation by taking into account the contract assumption, the trustee would be unable to establish this element of § 547.").

137. *See* Gonzales v. Sun Life Ins. Co. (*In re* Furr's Supermakets, Inc.), 485 B.R. 672 (Bankr. D. N.M. 2012) (constructing a series of six hypotheticals to examine whether there is preference liability under the assumption defense).

138. *See* Smith v. Creative Fin. Mgmt., Inc. (*In re* Virginia-Carolina Fin. Corp.), 954 F.2d 193, 199 (4th Cir. 1992) (analyzing guarantor defense by focusing "not on whether a creditor may have recovered all of the monies owed by the debtor from any source whatsoever, but instead upon whether the creditor would have received less than a 100% payout" from the bankruptcy estate).

apply as precisely in this situation. The trustee will argue that you were paid in full during the preference period with money that could have gone into a pot for unsecured creditors. It doesn't help unsecured creditors that, hypothetically, you would've been paid in full by a third-party in a hypothetical Chapter 7 case. The I-would've-been-paid-in-full-anyway justification is weaker, and some courts have rejected this defense.[139] Nonetheless, the argument does fit the letter of the law.

3.3 The Guilty-with-an-Explanation Defenses

The first line of defense is showing that the trustee has failed to prove what she needs to prove.[140] Unfortunately, she doesn't have a very high burden.[141] Most of the time, it's easy to show that you (the defendant) got the money, you were owed the money, the debtor is insolvent, and you got the money in the 90 days before the bankruptcy.[142] Proving this is not rocket science—intentionally so.

The trustee's light burden is precisely the intent of the "new" preference laws.[143] As shown earlier, the supreme goal is equality of treatment of unsecured creditors. Causing pain to preferred creditors is seen as a

---

139. *See* United Rentals, Inc. v. Angell, 592 F.3d 525 (4th Cir. 2010) (rejecting creditor's defense that "had the transfers not been made, [creditor] could have received full payment from the [third party guarantor] by enforcing its bond rights").

140. Rafael I. Pardo, *On Proof of Preferential Effect*, 55 Ala. L. Rev. 281, 286 (2004) ("The trustee has the burden to establish the avoidability of a transfer and the burden of pleading, proof, and persuasion with respect to all five elements of a preference. Once the trustee has established all the elements of a preference, the burden shifts to the transferee to establish one of the statutory defenses provided by the Code."); *see also* Boberschmidt v. Society Nat'l Bank (*In re* Jones), 226 F.3d 917, 921 (7th Cir. 2000) (stating that trustee bears the burden of proving the elements of section 547(b)).

141. Pardo, *supra* note 143, at 299 (opining that courts should not require "a more demanding burden of proof on the trustee than that required by the Code .... A court should not deny the trustee's avoidance power its full statutory reach, for to do so allows a creditor to be preferred, thereby eroding the equality principle"); *see also* Countryman, *supra* note 37, at 729 (stating that "in most cases, the creditor-defendant in a preference action makes no effort to rebut the section 547(f) presumption of the debtor's insolvency . . . and the presumption carries the day for the trustee or other party attacking the preference").

142. *Id.*

143. Hall, *supra* note 9, at 49 ("Congress' intention that unsecured creditors be better protected is manifest in the 1984 Amendments to the Code's preference provisions.").

reasonable price.[144] So, it's easy on purpose for trustees to bring clawback suits.[145]

Even so, Congress decided that certain exceptions to clawback prosecution should be retained. Since a preferential transfer is assumed in most cases, I facetiously call these the "guilty-with-an-explanation" defenses.

You're guilty, but you can walk if you have a good excuse.

These defenses are more correctly known as the "affirmative defenses." The most common affirmative defenses are

- the ordinary course defense,[146]

- the contemporaneous exchange defense, [147] and

- the subsequent new value defense.[148]

3.3.1 The Ordinary Course Defense

The most popular defense is the centuries-old ordinary course defense.[149]

---

144. *Id.* at 49-50 ("The three most significant changes in the preference provisions of Section 547 result in increased protection for unsecured creditors. First, Section 547(b)(4) has eliminated the requirement that the trustee show that an insider to whom a preferential transfer was made have had reasonable cause to know of the debtor's insolvency. Second, a transfer no longer must be made within forty-five days of the debt's incurrence in order to be sheltered by Section 547(c)(2). Third, Section 547(c)(7) prohibits avoidance of consumer transfers which constitute or affect property interests amounting to $600 or less.").

145. *Id.*

146. *See* 11 U.S.C. § 547(c)(2) ("The trustee may not avoid under this section a transfer . . . to the extent that such transfer was in payment of a debt incurred by the debtor in the ordinary course of business or financial affairs of the debtor and the transferee, and such transfer was—(A) made in the ordinary course of business or financial affairs of the debtor and the transferee; or (B) made according to ordinary business terms[.]").

147. *See* 11 U.S.C. § 547(c)(1) ("The trustee may not avoid under this section a transfer . . . to the extent that such transfer was—(A) intended by the debtor and the creditor to or for whose benefit such transfer was made to be a contemporaneous exchange for new value given to the debtor; and (B) in fact a substantially contemporaneous exchange[.]").

148. *See* 11 U.S.C. § 547(c)(4) ("The trustee may not avoid under this section a transfer . . . to or for the benefit of a creditor, to the extent that, after such transfer, such creditor gave new value to or for the benefit of the debtor— (A) not secured by an otherwise unavoidable security interest; and (B) on account of which new value the debtor did not make an otherwise unavoidable transfer to or for the benefit of such creditor[.]").

149. Brian Kotliar, Note: *A New Reading of the Ordinary Course of Business Exception in Section 547(c)(2)*, 21 Am. Bankr. Inst. L. Rev. 211, 212 (2013) ("No other preference defense has been litigated more than the ordinary course of business exception . . . ."); *see also* 11 U.S.C. § 547(c)(2) ("The trustee may not avoid under this section a transfer . . . to the extent that such transfer was in payment of a debt incurred by the debtor in the ordinary course of business or financial affairs of the debtor and the transferee, and such transfer was—(A) made in the ordinary course of business or financial affairs of the debtor and the transferee; or (B) made according to ordinary business terms[.]").

Laymen often confuse the ordinary course defense with the non-existent "I-know-nothing" defense.[150] When faced with a preference lawsuit, everybody's first impulse is to claim ignorance.

- "I didn't know the debtor would file for bankruptcy."

- "I didn't know other creditors were not paid."

- "I didn't know the debtor preferred me."

The reasoning is that if I knew nothing, then my intentions were innocent, and the payment must have been ordinary.[151]

The problem is that under the "new" (gutted) ordinary course defense, courts can't consider your intent or what you knew or didn't know.[152] What you intended or knew is theoretically irrelevant.

Ordinary is What Happened Before

Instead, courts figured out another way for folks to prove ordinariness.[153] With no direction from Congress, courts invented a brand-new intent-free ordinary course defense.[154]

The courts simply defined "ordinary" as meaning "the same as before."[155]

---

150. There is no such defense.

151. I call this the "Sgt. Schultz defense," after the Nazi guard in *Hogan's Heroes*, whose catchphrase was "I know nothing! Nothing!"

152. Ponoroff & Ashby, *supra* note 39, at 13 (stating that "the Code eschewed the "reasonable cause to believe" requirement that forced Act trustees to prove that the transferee-creditor knew or had reason to know of the debtor's insolvency as of the time the transfer occurred"); Kotliar, *supra* note 152, at 225 (stating that "the statute no longer contained the 'reasonable cause to believe' requirement for non-insider cases").

153. *Id.* at 213 (stating that "courts have been left to their own devices to interpret what exactly is in 'ordinary course of business' and what are 'ordinary business terms'").

154. Hall, *supra* note 9, at 71 (citing 129 Cong. Rec. S. 8897 (daily ed. June 29, 1984) (statements of Senators Dole and DeConcini) (stating that the exception "protects from avoidance transfers made in payment of debts incurred in the ordinary course of the parties' business . . . . Therefore, if the creditor can prove that the transfer meets 'ordinary business' criteria, the transfer will remain intact.")); *see also* Fortgang & King, *The 1978 Bankruptcy Code: Some Wrong Policy Decisions*, 56 N.Y.U. L. Rev. 1148, 1167-70 (1981).

155. Herbert, *supra* note 8, at 205 ("The courts have almost unanimously required that for the transfer to be in the ordinary course of business, it must be 'subjectively' in the ordinary course of business—that is, it must be in conformity with the prior dealings of the parties."); *see also In re* Economy Milling Co., Inc., 37 B.R. 914, 922 (D. S.C. 1983) (finding that the creditor "need only to have shown that he, or other farmers had entered into like option contracts with the debtor in the past").

If payment by the debtor to a creditor during the 90-day preference period was made in a manner consistent with payments made in a past "business as usual" time period, then the payment is "ordinary" and cannot be clawed back.

It works like this:

First, the court observes how the debtor and vendor acted during the 90 days before the bankruptcy. Did the debtor pay late or on time? Did the debtor pay by wire or regular mail? Was there collection pressure?

Second, the court compares that conduct to how the parties acted during a "normal" time period before the 90-day preference period. If the parties acted the same during the "normal" period and the preference period, the conduct during the preference period is deemed "ordinary." That's all there is to it.[156]

A debtor in a "normal" time, way before the bankruptcy, always paid invoices in 110 days, and only after being threatened with a lawsuit. Fast forward to the 90-day preference period right before the bankruptcy. The same debtor still pays in 110 days and still only after a lawsuit threat. That sameness is evidence of "ordinariness." Maybe this is not "ordinary" for most companies and vendors. It doesn't matter. It is "ordinary" for the parties in the context of a preference defense because this is how these folks always did business.[157]

There's no need to decipher anybody's intent. No listening to self-serving statements by defendants. No need to read anyone's mind. The considerable advantage of this definition of ordinariness is that the analysis can be boiled down to numbers and statistics, and often is.

---

156. Deborah L. Thorne, *Lien on Me:, [sic] Reexamining the Ordinary Course Defense: A Multifactor Approach*, 32-11 ABI J. 32, 83 (2013) (examining a number of different factors regarding prior conduct of the parties to determine whether the transfers received during the preference period were consistent with the pre-preference period transfers (citing Burtch v. Texstars Inc. (*In re* AE Liquidation Inc.), 2013 WL 5488476 (Bankr. D. Del. 2013))).

157. Ponoroff & Ashby, *supra* note 39, at 18 (stating that the object of the ordinary business exception is to "protect recurring, customary credit transactions that would have taken place in the ordinary course of the debtor's and creditor's businesses regardless of whether the prospect of a bankruptcy was looming or not").

Factors That Show Normalcy

Now that the courts had defined "ordinary course" conduct as that consistent with behavior in a "normal" time, the courts had to decide what exact conduct is most relevant.

When the debtor's business was good, way before the bankruptcy, the owner would wear a red tie and meet the vendor personally at Starbucks to hand over a payment check. In the preference period, right before the bankruptcy, the debtor met the vendor at *McDonald's* and wore a *blue* tie when he paid an invoice.

Clearly, the deviation in choice of tie color or restaurant should not be counted as evidence that the parties acted out of the ordinary course during the preference period.

In deciding what variables are relevant, the courts focus on behaviors that seem to be connected to whether there was favoritism or attempts to gain an advantage on the eve of a bankruptcy.

The primary conduct the courts consider is how long the debtor took to pay invoices and whether that changed. Courts look at "days outstanding"—the number of days that elapses between sending an invoice and getting paid.

If a debtor pays a vendor within the same time frame after receiving an invoice—neither later nor earlier—both in a "normal" period and right before a bankruptcy, this is considered evidence that neither the debtor nor the vendor made any special effort to favor the vendor. The vendor just happened to get paid on bankruptcy eve.

Proving Nothing

Proving a negative—lack of change, or "nothing"—is what the ordinary course defense requires.[158]

The vendor must prove that nothing changed in the transition from the "normal" period to the eve-of-bankruptcy period.

The courts accept data derived from all kinds of statistical methodol-

---

158. It's the "Jerry Seinfeld defense." It's all about nothing.

ogies as evidence that nothing changed. Courts consider averages of days outstanding, weighted averages, standard deviation analysis, and "bucketing" analysis.

Courts have succeeded in replacing sticky intent with clean statistical analysis![159]

Or have they...?

3.3.1.1 The Problems with the Ordinary Course Defense

Fails to Protect Most Ordinary Conduct

As described below, the ordinary course defense is not about ordinary conduct in the usual sense of the word "ordinary."

You might argue that it's "ordinary" for folks to pay later when they are in financial distress.[160] You might argue that it's "ordinary" to extend payment terms to a struggling client or customer.[161] You could also argue that it's "ordinary" to start ramping up your collection efforts when a customer is paying later and later.[162]

These arguments have all been shot down. The sole consideration for courts is consistency. Changes with good explanations are generally not acceptable and may destroy the ordinary course defense.

So the first problem with the ordinary course defense is that it fails to protect most ordinary course conduct.

---

159. Herbert, *supra* note 8, at 207-08 (1985) (stating that "most courts . . . have adopted the subjective standard, which has led to the rule that any behavioral change between the parties indicates that the transfer is not in the ordinary course of business, even if the mode of transfer or the terms under which it was made are not abnormal").

160. *In re* Tolona Pizza Prods. Corp., 3 F.3d 1029, 1032 (7th Cir. 1993) (explaining that a payment that is made beyond invoice or contract terms may still be considered in the ordinary course if late payments were the standard course of dealing between the parties).

161. Grogan v. Liberty Nat'l Life Ins. Co. (*In re* Advance Glove Mfg. Co.), 761 F.2d 249, 251 (6th Cir. 1985) (stating that Congress enacted 547(c)(2) "'to leave undisturbed normal financial relations, because it does not detract from the general policy of the preference section to discourage unusual action by either the debtor or his creditors during the debtor's slide into bankruptcy'" (quoting S. Rep. No. 989, 95th Cong., 2d Sess. 88 (1978))); *see also* Yurika Foods Corp. v. United Parcel Serv. (*In re* Yurika Foods Corp.), 888 F.2d 42, 44 (6th Cir. 1989) ("Even if the debtor's business transactions were irregular, they may be considered "ordinary" for purposes of section 547(c)(2) if those transactions were consistent with the course of dealings between the particular parties." (quoting *In re* Fulghum Const. Corp., 872 F.2d 739, 743 (6th Cir. 1989))).

162. *Id.*

Still Intent Based

The defense purports to be based on hard facts and measurable conduct. However, those facts and conduct are really only marshaled to imply a lack of preferential intent.

The difference from the past law is that courts now focus on a particular form of circumstantial evidence of preferential intent or lack thereof.[163]

Consider the following example.

Jones constantly threatened lawsuits and demanded wire transfers both during the five years before the preference period and during the preference period. The day before the bankruptcy he demands an immediate wire transfer. Jones might well have an ordinary course defense since his conduct is consistent with past behavior.

Smith also insists on a wire the day before the bankruptcy. However, Smith never made such a demand before. He likely has no ordinary course defense.

The same conduct, demanding a wire, might be excused in the first case and punished in the second case. Why?

A judge might view Jones's wire demand as unconnected to the imminent bankruptcy since Jones had been making the same demand for years. On the other hand, the court may well deduce that Smith's out of character demand was motivated by the looming bankruptcy threat.

- Two vendors.

- Both demand wires.

- Both get paid while the debtor is insolvent

- Both get paid in full

- Both leave other creditors to split a tiny pie

---

163. 5-547 *Collier on Bankruptcy* 547.04[2][a][ii] (16th ed. 2016) ("There is no precise legal test that can be applied in determining whether payments by the debtor during the 90-day period were made in the ordinary course of business; 'rather, the court must engage in a subjective "peculiarly factual" analysis.'"(quoting Lovett v. St. Johnsbury Trucking, 931 F.2d 494, 497 (8th Cir. 1991))).

- Both diminish the estate

But only one is defensible.

The only difference is that Jones seemed to lack the specific intent to obtain preferential treatment before a bankruptcy and maybe Smith had such intent.

The laws' focus on consistency serves an ancient purpose—to protect creditors with innocent intent and punish those with preferential intent.

The problem is that while the consistency paradigm might sometimes weed out vendors with bad intent, it fails in many cases to protect those with good intent. With this automatic rule, there is no room for subtlety.

Smith might well have wanted to scoop the bankruptcy. Or he might have had no clue about the looming bankruptcy. He may have demanded a wire because his mother's required an urgent operation. The "new" preference laws, being formula based, are blind to valid exceptions.

The Problem with Relying on Lack of Change

While the *absence* of change might indicate a lack of preferential intent, the *presence* of change does not prove preferential intent.

Your long-term customer asks for extended terms since he's having some "temporary" financial issues. You let him pay in 60 days instead of 30 days. He goes bankrupt two months later. Your conduct in accepting a 60-days term during the preference period would be found to be inconsistent with your past behavior.

The above scenario is an example of a change that may destroy the ordinary course defense. That change, though, is not proof that any particular effort was made by either you or the debtor to parcel out special treatment.

Limiting the ordinary course defense to an inflexible change/no change rule eliminates the difficulty and expense of proving or defending intent. It also brings in a ton of clawback money. The price is a general sense of unfairness, arbitrariness and the punishment of many (if not most) accidental recipients of preferential transfers.

Are the current preference laws worth the price? I give my two cents in part 6.

3.3.1.2 How to Present This Defense

Despite the rote recitation in textbooks that the court considers many factors in applying the ordinary course defense and that each case is unique, the defense often rests on a small number of statistics. Either you have the right numbers, or you don't. The mechanical nature of the defense can be an advantage.

First, if you do have the right numbers, the plaintiff may quickly agree to dismiss the clawback lawsuit.

Second, dependence on statistics eliminates most factual disputes. Both sides have the same evidence showing when the debtor paid invoices. So, the central piece of evidence is often undisputed. The problem with "he said/she said" factual disputes is that they lead to a lot of document exchanges, depositions, trials—and cost. The courts' reliance on statistics removes a considerable litigation expense.

Courts compare the "days outstanding" (days elapsed from date of invoice to receipt of check) in the "base" (also known as "comparison") period to the days outstanding in the preference period. The analysis is done in a few separate ways:

- comparing averages[164]

- comparing weighted averages[165]

---

164. *See* Kapila v. Media Buying, Inc. (*In re* Ameri P.O.S., Inc.), 355 B.R. 876, 884 (Bankr. S.D. Fla. 2006) (noting that one approach to calculating a baseline is to "calculate the average lag-time between invoice and payment").

165. William B. Johnson, *Timing of Transfer as Being in "Ordinary Course of Business or Financial Affairs" for Purposes of 11 U.S.C.A. § 547(c)(2)(A) — Chapter 7 Cases*, 75 A.L.R. Fed. 2d 93 (citing *In re* Lan Yik Foods Corp., 185 B.R. 103 (Bankr. E.D.N.Y. 1995) (using weighted average method to calculate time periods if an invoice was paid with more than one payment, whereby the ratio of each individual payment to the invoice total was multiplied by the number of days from the invoice date to the payment date)); *see also* Unsecured Creds. Comm. v. Jason's Foods, Inc. (*In re* Sparrer Sausage Co., Inc.), 2014 Bankr. LEXIS 3661 (Bankr. N.D. Ill. 2014) (using weighted average method for the baseline period and comparing that to the average payment gap of the invoices during the preference period); Davis v. Clarklift West, Inc. (*In re* Quebecor World (USA), Inc.), 518 B.R. 757 (Bankr. S.D.N.Y. 2014) (weighted average payment gap of 77.79 days during the preference period versus 50.29 days prior to the preference period were preferential).

- comparing ranges[166]

- comparing "buckets"[167]

- the standard deviation[168]

3.3.1.2.1 Comparing Averages

The simplest way of showing consistency between base period days out-standing and preference period days outstanding is to compare averages. Let's expand our hypothetical.

- Curly ran a car wash. After each car wash, he would send Moe an invoice with 30-day terms.

- In the year before the preference period, Curly washed Moe's car three times.

- He got paid $50.00 in 30 days for the first wash, $50.00 in 45 days for the second wash, and $50.00 in 54 days for the last wash.

- During the 90 days before the bankruptcy (the preference period), Curly washed Moe's car twice and got paid in 55 days for each wash.

A trustee sues Curly for the return of the alleged preferences. He hires me to represent him.

3.3.1.2.2 Simple Average Comparison

First, I take a simple average of the payments during the comparison, or "base," period. The average is 45 days. The average "days outstand-ing," defined as the time between the invoice date and payment, in the

---

166. *See In re Ameri P.O.S., Inc.*, 355 B.R. at 884 (citing *In re* Home Sewing Enter, Inc., 173 B.R. 782, 788 (N.D. Ga. 1993)) (noting that one approach to calculating a baseline is to "establish a 'range' within which transactions were consummated").

167. Ponoroff, *supra* note 37, at 361 (2016) (rejecting defendant's "total range" approach and adopting an "average late-ness" method, calling for the grouping of payments into individual "buckets" by age, and then analyzing to determine the percentage of the historical payments falling into each bucket (citing *In re* Davis v. R.A. Brooks Trucking Co., Inc. (*In re* Quebecor World (USA), Inc.) , 491 B.R. 379 (Bankr. S.D.N.Y. 2013))).

168. Gregory S. Abrams, Joseph L. Steinfeld Jr., & Joseph A. Hess, *Prosecuting Preference Actions Post-BAPCPA: Another View Toward a Reliable Statistical Model*, 25-10 ABI J. 54, 108 n.5 (2006) (describing how to measure standard deviation to determine veracity of "ordinary course of business" defense).

preference period is obviously 55 days. Moe paid Curly 10 days later, on average, during the preference period.

As we have seen, the courts define ordinariness as consistency.[169] But there is *no* bright line rule as to how much consistency is required.[170] Some courts say that anything under a 20% change in average days outstanding might be consistent enough to be considered ordinary.[171] If Curly got paid in 90 days in the last couple of prebankruptcy months, he probably would not have an ordinary course defense. Payments made in 90 days would be considered "non-ordinary" as compared with the base period's 45-day average.

3.3.1.2.3 Weighted Average Comparison

I email the trustee and ask her to dismiss the case because the averages are so close. She points out that the *weighted* averages comparison is not as favorable to Curly.

In simple terms, it might be misleading to give the payment timing of a small invoice the same weight as the payment timing of a large invoice. For example, if the debtor paid a $5 invoice in 30 days and a $500,000 invoice in 60 days, the larger invoice payment timing should be given more weight in determining what is ordinary.

A weighted average is obtained when each quantity to be averaged is assigned a weight so that all quantities do not have the same effect on (or importance to) the average. In the bankruptcy preference context, a weighted average of the number of days it took for invoices to be paid is

---

169. *See* Gasmark Ltd. Liquidating Trust v. Louis Dreyfus Natural Gas Corp., 158 F.3d 312, 317 (5th Cir. 1998) (stating analysis focuses on whether timing of payments was consistent with ordinary practice between debtor and creditor); *see also Lovett*, 931 F.2d at 499 (8th Cir. 1991) (holding that a payment was made according to ordinary business terms because the manner, form, and timing of these payments were consistent with the practice both parties followed).

170. 5-547 *Collier on Bankruptcy* 547.04[2][a][ii] (16th ed. 2016) ("To determine whether a late payment may still be considered ordinary between the parties, a court will normally compare the degree of lateness of each of the alleged preferences with the pattern of payments before the preference period to see if the alleged preferences fall within that pattern.").

171. *See* Cox v. Momar Inc. (*In re* Affiliated Foods Southwest Inc.), 750 F.3d 714, 721 (8th Cir. 2014) (a payment made 26 days after the invoice was not preferential when, in the two-year period preceding the section 547 lookback period, the average gap was 35 days and the range was 13 to 49 days); *see also* Goodman v. Candy Fleet, LLC (*In re* Gulf Fleet Holdings, Inc.), 2014 Bankr. LEXIS 1123 (Bankr. W.D. La. 2014) (rejecting this defense when the average payment gap during the preference period was 22.5 days while it had been 13 days in prior dealings).

calculated as follows. One multiplies each invoice amount by the number of days it took for it to be paid and then divides the sum of those values by the total dollar amount of the invoices in the data set.[172]

For example, see tables 1 and 2:

TABLE 1. Weighted Average Comparison—Base Period

Invoice Date	Invoice Amount	Payment Date	Check Amount	Days to Pay	Weightings
11/16/12	$8,580.00	01/18/13	$8,580.00	63.00	540,540
11/30/12	$5,200.00	02/18/13	$13,260.00	80.00	416,000
12/15/12	$8,060.00	02/18/13		65.00	523,900
Total				208.00	1,480,440
Average (208 ÷ 3)				69.33	
Weighted Average (1,480,440 ÷ 21,840)				67.79	

TABLE 2. Weighted Average Comparison—Preference Period

Invoice Date	Invoice Amount	Payment Date	Check Amount	Days to Pay	Weightings
02/16/13	$910.00	04/07/13	$910.00	50.00	45,500.00
03/01/13	$9,100.00	06/06/13	$30,845.00	97.00	882,700.00
03/16/13	$13,840.00	06/06/13	$30,845.00	82.00	1,134,880.00
04/01/13	$7,905.00	06/06/13		66.00	521,730.00
Total	$31,755.00			295.00	2,584,810
Average (204 ÷ 4)				73.75	
Weighted Average (2,584,810 ÷ 31,755)				81.40	

In this example, the weighted average rose from 67.79 days during the base period to 81.40 days during the preference period.

While there was only a 4.42 days difference in the simple averages from the base period to the preference period (a 6.37% increase), the difference in the weighted averages was much larger; i.e., a 13.61 days difference (a 20.07% increase).

172. *In re* Forklift LP Corp., 2006 US Dist. Lexis 50264.

3.3.1.2.4 Ranges

The problem with comparing averages is that there could be some payments in the preference period made extremely late, and others made unusually early, but the average of all payments in the preference period could be the same as that in the base period.[173] That is, the average for the preference period and the base period could be the same, but the actual payment timings of individual invoices could be wildly different. For example, 12 payments in the base period were each made in 62.5 days. The two payments made during the preference period were made in 25 days and 100 days, for an average of 62.5 days outstanding. In this situation, a trustee might argue that comparing averages is false evidence of consistency.

The Bankruptcy Code does not provide exceptions for groups of transfers during the preference period. It only provides a defense for each transfer. Courts cannot take a big-picture view and excuse all preference period transfers because the aggregate average is the same as the aggregate average in the base period. Courts must consider each payment received during the preference period and decide whether that *particular* payment was "ordinary" or "non-ordinary."[174] So, especially in the case where the individual transfers are dramatically earlier or later in the preference period, a comparison of the averages will probably not convince a judge of ordinariness.[175]

Another way of showing ordinariness—and don't forget it's *our* burden to show it and prove it, *not* the trustee's burden—is the "range" analysis.[176]

---

173. Moltech Power Sys. v. Tooh Dineh Indus., Inc. (*In re* Moltech Power Sys., Inc.), 327 B.R. 675, 681 (Bankr. N.D. Fla. 2005) (noting that "courts have stated that averages alone can be misleading because they do not take into account seasonal variations and other considerations, resulting in inaccurate depictions of what the ordinary course of business actually was" (citing *In re* Speco Corp., 218 B.R. 390, 399 (Bankr. S.D. Ohio 1998), and Gonzales v. DPI Food Prods. Co. (*In re* Furrs Supermarkets, Inc.), 296 B.R. 33, 44 (Bankr. D. N.M. 2003))).

174. *See Lovett*, 931 F.2d at 497 (stating that "th[e] court must engage in a subjective "peculiarly factual" analysis" to determine whether a payment was ordinary or non-ordinary (quoting *In re Fulghum Constr. Corp.*, 872 F.2d at 743)).

175. Ellenberg v. Tulip Prod. Polymerics, Inc. (*In re* T.B. Home Sewing Enters., Inc.), 173 B.R. 782, 788-89 (Bankr. N.D. Ga. 1993) (conducting a range analysis where payments to defendant occurred anywhere between 27 to 176 days after the invoice date); *see also* Jensen v. Raymond Bldg. Supply Corp. (*In re* Homes of Port Charlotte Florida, Inc.), 109 B.R. 489 (Bankr. M.D. Fla. 1990).

176. *Id.*

The range analysis involves comparing two "ranges" of numbers.[177] The first range is the earliest payment to the latest payment in the base period.[178] The second range, of course, is the earliest payment to the latest payment in the preference period.[179]

If Moe paid Curly in the base period in a range of 10 days to 45 days and then paid him in the preference period in a range of 15 days to 30 days, then Curly was paid "within range." The payments in the preference period were within range because they were all made after 10 days and before 45 days.

The theory here is that the payments in the preference period were ordinary because they were made neither earlier nor later than other "normal" payments in the parties' history.

The argument is: "We've seen this before between the parties." This is "business as usual," not inconsistent with the way these parties did business before the preference period.

As an example, see tables 3 and 4:

TABLE 3. Ranges—Base Period

Invoice No.	Invoice Amount	Invoice Date	Payment Date	Days to Pay
3107	$176.00	5/9/11	6/20/11	42
3529	$274.00	6/30/11	10/17/11	109
3658	$836.00	7/28/11	10/17/11	81
3762	$310.00	8/19/11	10/17/11	59
3911	$2,785.00	8/31/11	10/17/11	47
3914	$1,104.00	8/31/11	11/26/11	87
3915	$1,139.00	8/31/11	12/20/11	111
3917	$1,080.00	8/31/11	12/18/11	109
Least Number of Days				42
Most Number of Days				111
Range of Payments				42–111

---

177. *Id.; see also In re Moltech Power Sys., Inc.*, 327 B.R. at 681 (stating that "the range established before the preference period should be comparable to the range of payment terms during the preference period on both the low and high end to ensure that the range is not skewed by aberrational transactions").

178. *Id.*

179. *Id.*

TABLE 4. Ranges—Preference Period

Invoice No.	Amount	Invoice Date	Payment Date	Days to Pay	Comparison to the Base Period Range of Payments
4079	$1,403.00	09/30/11	02/13/12	136	out of range
4433	$915.00	11/30/11	02/13/12	75	within range
4605	$895.00	12/29/11	04/04/12	97	within range
Least Number of Days				75	
Most Number of Days				136	
Range of Payments				75–136	

Here, the range of payments during the base period is 42–111 days. The range during the preference period is 75–136 days. Therefore, the first payment, which was 136 days late, is out of the 42–111 days range established during the base period and might be considered non-ordinary. The other two payments made 75 days and 97 days after the invoice date, are within the range and so might be regarded as ordinary.

3.3.1.2.5 Comparing Buckets

The "bucketing" analysis addresses a situation that averages and ranges do not.

Let's say that the average payment days outstanding is identical in the base period and the preference period. Let's further assume that all the payments received in the preference period were made within the same range as in the base period. There still may be a situation where the trustee can convince the judge that payments in the preference period were not ordinary.

Let's change the Curly hypothetical once more. Let's assume the following facts:

- Moe made 50 payments to Curly during the base period.

- These payments were made between 25 days and 70 days after the invoice date.

- In the preference period, Moe paid Curly five times, always in 65 days.

- So, all payments in the preference period were "within range" of payments made in the base period.

- But let's also assume that Moe paid in 70 days *only once* in the entire one-year base period. All the other payments were made in 25 to 30 days.

I email the trustee and ask for dismissal. The trustee emails back and says that while he agrees that the payments in the preference period were "within range," the range analysis fails to prove ordinariness. He claims the analysis is misleading because the 70-days payment was an "outlier" since only one payment was made that late, and the "true" range is 25 to 30 days with the outlier removed.

The trustee then applies the "bucketing" analysis.

The trustee says that the number of payments made by Moe to Curly in the "bucket" of payments made between 30 and 60 days during the base period was over 90% of the payments, and only 1% were paid in the 61–90-days "bucket." The trustee points out that in the preference period, by comparison, Moe made 0% of his payments during the 0–30-days "bucket" and 100% of his payments in the 61–90-days "bucket."

To summarize, the bucketing analysis breaks down the base period into 30-day "buckets."[180] The typical buckets are 30 day ranges from 0 to 30, 31 to 60, 61 to 90, and over 90.[181] The trustee will calculate the percentage of payments in each bucket and compare each bucket to the corresponding buckets and percentages in the preference period.[182]

180. Davis v. R.A. Brooks Trucking Co., Inc. (*In re* Quebecor World (USA), Inc.), 491 B.R. 379, 388 (Bankr. S.D.N.Y. 2013) ("In deciding what payments are ordinary, a court reviews the range of payments centered around the average and also groups the payments in buckets by age." (citing Hechinger Inv. Co. of Delaware, Inc. v. Universal Forest Prods., Inc. (*In re* Hechinger Inv. Co. of Delaware, Inc.), 489 F.3d 568, 578 (3d Cir. 2007))).

181. U.S. Bank Nat'l Ass'n v. Spectra Mktg. Sys. (*In re* Interstate Bakeries Corp.), Nos. 04-45814, 09-4177, 2011 Bankr. LEXIS 140 (Bankr. W.D. Mo. 2011) (featuring defendant in preference action who uses "bucketing" and insists "that the collection practices in the industry are based on a 30-day 'bucket' system, whereby accounts are categorized according to whether they are paid between 0-30, 31-60, 61-90, or 90 days past invoice date and that collection calls are placed only after an account is 90 days past due").

182. Mark Fisher, *7th Circ. Provides Road Map for Preference Defendants*, Law360, https://www.law360.com/ articles/811325/7th-circ-provides-road-map-for-preference-defendants (June 27, 2016) (citing Unsecured Creditors

The trustee argues that comparing the averages and ranges can be deceptive if there are outliers that skew the average or range within a particular period. The trustee will say that in such a situation, bucketing provides a more in-depth and realistic analysis.

As an example, let's look at tables 5, 6 and 7:

TABLE 5. Bucketing—Base Period

Invoice Date	Invoice Amount	Payment Amount	Payment Date	Days to Pay
11/23/11	$451.20	$451.20	02/20/12	89
12/01/11	$90.24	$90.24	02/20/12	81
04/11/12	$1,071.60	$1,071.60	06/04/12	54
11/07/12	$676.80	$676.80	12/05/12	28
09/19/12	$1,051.02	$1,051.02	11/05/12	47
09/26/12	$1,046.72	$1,046.72	11/05/12	40
10/03/12	$1,029.27	$1,029.27	11/05/12	33
10/10/12	$1,037.58	$1,037.58	12/05/12	56
10/31/12	$1,255.73	$1,255.73	12/05/12	35
11/07/12	$1,392.75	$1,392.75	12/11/12	34

TABLE 6. Bucketing—Preference Period

Invoice Date	Invoice Amount	Payment Amount	Payment Date	Days to Pay
11/14/12	$490.68	$490.68	01/16/13	63
12/12/12	$1,252.87	$1,252.87	01/16/13	35
12/19/12	$1,574.41	$1,574.41	02/25/13	68
01/03/13	$34.98	$34.98	02/25/13	53
01/03/13	$460.42	$460.42	02/25/13	53
01/09/13	$427.42	$427.42	02/25/13	47

Comm. of Sparrer Sausage Co., Inc. v. Jason's Foods, Inc., 826 F.3d 388 (7th Cir. 2016)) (stating that the "court said that the "bucket approach" is one appropriate method to defining the ordinary course based on a spread of days from the average payment period . . . . Hence, the range of all payments during the historical period may be considered ordinary course if they are tightly distributed without substantial outliers."))

TABLE 7. Bucketing Analysis

Buckets	Base Period		Preference Period	
0 to 30 days	1	10.00%	0	0.00%
31 to 60 days	7	70.00%	4	66.67%
61 to 90 days	2	20.00%	2	33.33%
Total Number of Payments	10	100.00%	6	100.00%

Figure 1. Bucketing—Base Period   **Figure 2. Bucketing—Preference Period**

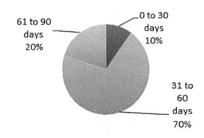
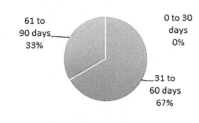

In the example above, most payments during the base period were made within the bucket range of 31–60 days. During the preference period, most payments were also made within the bucket range of 31–60 days, which would make these payments ordinary.

3.3.1.2.6 Standard Deviation

Some courts have embraced standard deviation statistical analysis to determine ordinariness.

Standard deviation measures statistical dispersion. It shows how spread-out a set of values is around the mean of that set of values.[183] In the bankruptcy preference context, it allows us to view the payments centered around the mean.[184] This analysis measures how much variation in the days outstanding is to be expected from the average days outstanding. When the standard deviation number is applied to both sides of the mean

---

183. Abrams, Steinfeld, & Hess, *supra* note 171, at 108 n.5 ("A 'standard deviation' is a statistical measure of the amount by which a set of values differs from the arithmetical mean.").

184. Pereira v. United Parcel Service of America, Inc. a/k/a UPS (*In re* Waterford Wedgewood USA, Inc.), 508 B.R. 821, 836 (Bankr. S.D.N.Y. 2014) ("Similar to the average lateness method, a standard deviation analysis serves to view the payments centered around the mean.").

or average during the base period, the payments during the preference period that fall within the resulting range may be ordinary.[185]

Let's assume that the average during the base period is 45 days and the standard deviation of all the payments made during the base period is 6. Then, the standard deviation range would be 39 (45 days – 6) to 51 (45 days + 6). So, all the payments during the preference period that were made within 39 to 51 days would be ordinary.

Using the same example, +/-6 is one standard deviation; two standard deviations is +/- 12 (6 x 2), three standard deviations is +/- 18 (6 x 3), and so on. Courts have held that all transfers falling within one standard deviation of the base period average should be considered as having made consistent with the parties' ordinary business terms.[186]

3.3.1.2.7 Other Factors

Courts may turn to other kinds of evidence of "ordinariness." However, "ordinariness" is always defined as conduct consistent with past conduct.[187]

As seen above, Courts' hyper-focus on consistency with the past seems to blind them to other evidence of ordinariness. For example:

- It's ordinary for a creditor to extend terms to troubled customers and accept overdue payments. This is entirely "ordinary" conduct in the real world. Notwithstanding, courts will focus only on the fact that delinquent payments were made inconsistently with a year before, and ignore any other form of "ordinariness" as irrelevant.[188]

---

185. Abrams, Steinfeld, & Hess, *supra* note 171, at 108 n.5 (explaining that "when the standard deviation number is applied to both sides of the mean, the numbers that fall within the resulting range will encompass 67.76 percent of all numbers used to arrive at the mean").

186. *See In re Waterford Wedgewood USA, Inc.*, 508 B.R. at 837 (adopting trustee's use of one standard deviation from the mean).

187. Burtch v. Texstars, Inc. (*In re* AE Liquidation), 70 C.B.C. 2d 755, 203 Bankr. LEXIS 4144, at *9-10 (Bankr. D. Del. 2013) ("Courts have considered several factors in determining such consistency: (1) the length of time the parties engaged in the type of dealing at issue; (2) whether the subject transfers were in an amount more than usually paid; (3) whether the payments at issue were tendered in a manner different from previous payments; (4) whether there appears to have been an unusual action by the creditor or debtor to collect on or pay the debt; and (5) whether the creditor did anything to gain an advantage (such as obtain additional security) in light of the debtor's deteriorating financial condition.").

188. 5-547 *Collier on Bankruptcy* 547.04[2][a][ii] (16th ed. 2016) (stating that courts focus on "the degree of lateness of

- The debtor lost an invoice and ended up paying it 14 days late since it took time for the debtor to notice and for the creditor to send another invoice. This is ordinary in every business. The courts might ignore the explanation and simply focus on the lateness as being inconsistent with the past and, therefore, non-ordinary.[189]

Courts tend to weigh the following factors to determine consistency or inconsistency between the base period and the preference period:

- collection activity[190]

- form of payment[191]

- multiple payments of invoices[192]

- payments on account[193]

- proximity to the bankruptcy[194]

We will review each factor below.

---

each of the alleged preferences with the pattern of payments before the preference period to see if the alleged preferences fall within that pattern").

189. Logan v. Basic Distrib. Corp. (*In re* Fred Hawes Org., Inc.), 957 F.2d 239, 244 (6th Cir. 1992) ("A late payment will be considered 'ordinary' only upon a showing that late payments were the normal course of business between the parties.").

190. 5-547 *Collier on Bankruptcy* 547.04[2][a][ii] (16th ed. 2016) ("Payments made in response to 'unusual' debt collection practices by the creditor are outside the scope of ordinary course of business." (citing Marathon Oil Co. v. Flatau (*In re* Craig Oil Co.), 785 F.2d 1563 (11th Cir. 1986))); *see also* Bender Shipbuilding and Repair Co. v. Oil Recovery Co. Inc. of Alabama (*In re* Bender Shipbuilding and Repair Co.), 479 B.R. 899, 905 (Bankr. S.D. Ala. 2012) (stating that threat to discontinue supplying services to debtor unless overdue invoices paid was an unusual collection practice).

191. 5-547 *Collier on Bankruptcy* 547.04[2][a][ii] (16th ed. 2016) ("A sufficient pattern of similar types of payments before the preference period must be shown in order to prevail" in an ordinary course of business defense) (citing Central Hardware Co. v. Sherman-Williams Co. (*In re* Spirit Holding Co., Inc.), 153 F.3d 902 (8th Cir. 1998))).

192. *See* Webster v. Management Network Group, Inc. (*In re* Nettel Corp., Inc.), 364 B.R. 433, 449 (Bankr. D. D.C. 2006) (rejecting ordinary course of business defense where debtor waited much longer on average to pay off the invoices that were eventually paid in the preference period, and then made many more payments than it had in the past to satisfy those debts—including multiple installments on single invoices).

193. *See* Ames Merch. Corp. v. Cellmark Paper Inc. (*In re* Ames Dep't Stores, Inc.), 450 B.R. 24 (Bankr. S.D.N.Y. 2011) (rejecting ordinary course defense because "lump sum or partial payments" made by debtor were not consistent with the parties' payment scheme before preferential period).

194. *See* Fiber Lite Corp. v. Molded Acoustical Prods., Inc. (*In re* Molded Acoustical Prods., Inc.), 18 F.3d. 217, 219 (3d Cir. 1994) ("The ordinary course exception . . . "is formulated to induce creditors to continue dealing with a distressed debtor" even in proximity to the bankruptcy "so as to kindle its chances of survival without a costly detour through, or a humbling ending in, the sticky web of bankruptcy.").

3.3.1.2.7.1 Collection Activity

Courts often zero in on the rise in collection pressure as a crucial factor separating ordinary from non-ordinary prebankruptcy conduct.[195] Many judges will consider unusual collection pressure as a determinative factor even if the collection pressure did not result in an earlier or later payment.[196]

Some bankruptcy judges refuse to consider collection pressure if the payments themselves were not later or earlier compared with the base period.[197] This appears to be the minority view.

The disparity between these two positions is instructive. To repeat—the hypothetical payment pattern is itself unchanged; i.e., the preference period is consistent with the base period, but the creditor applied unusual collection pressure.

On the one hand, there is no circumstantial evidence that the debtor intended to and did prefer this particular creditor—the debtor paid within the same time frame it had always paid.

On the other hand, there seems to be circumstantial evidence that the creditor intended to obtain preferential treatment since it applied unusual collection pressure right before the bankruptcy.

If the law is to be applied with consistent logic, then consistency between the preference period and the base period should be the end of the story. But some courts disallow an ordinary course defense when

---

195. 5-547 *Collier on Bankruptcy* 547.04[2][a][ii] (16th ed. 2016) (stating that "whenever the bankruptcy court receives evidence of unusual collection efforts, it must consider whether the debtor's payment was in fact, a response to those efforts" (citing Marathon Oil Co. v. Flatau (*In re* Craig Oil Co.), 785 F.2d 1563 (11th Cir. 1986))).

196. *Id.* (stating that instead of looking at effect, courts will "normally compare the collection activities that preceded each challenged transfer with the pattern of collection activities occurring prior to the preference period to see if the collection activities that preceded the alleged preferences fall within that pattern").

197. *Id.* ("In many circumstances, a phone call or two demanding an overdue payment or threatening to delay further deliveries until overdue payments are made may be ordinary between the parties." (citing Sparkman v. Martin Marietta Materials, Inc. (*In re* Mainline Contracting, Inc.), 68 C.B.C. 2d 736, 2012 Bankr. LEXIS 4986, at *25-26 (Bankr. E.D.N.C. 2012))); *see also* Grant v. Suntrust Bank, Central Florida, N.A. (*In re* L. Bee Furniture Co., Inc.), 203 B.R. 778, 782 (Bankr. M.D. Fla. 1996).

there is consistency if there was also unusual collection pressure.[198, 199]

The rationale of these court opinions seems to be as follows. We won't allow the ordinary course defense if the creditor seemed to have had the *intent*—as shown by the heightened collection pressure—to be preferred. There is no other reason to consider creditor pressure that had no apparent impact on the debtor payment practices.

However, if we consider evidence of bad creditor intent; i.e., an intent to get preferential treatment, we should also recognize proof of *good* intent or lack of bad intent. But courts refuse to consider good intent.[200] For example, as seen above, a creditor's good intention in accepting past due payments through a workout agreement is irrelevant, and that conduct may be harmful to the ordinary course defense.[201]

A *trustee* can win by showing bad intent—collection pressure by a creditor even when the collection pressure had no preferential effect. But a *vendor* cannot defend by showing good intent—agreeing to accept later payments.

3.3.1.2.7.1.1   Practical Skinny on This Factor

Consistency of Collection Pressure

If there were collection pressure in the preference period, then you must, as a defense, identify examples of similar collection pressure in the base period.[202] Remember, what's ordinary is what happened before. If the

---

198. *Id.* ("The more intense the collection activity during the preference period the greater the likelihood that the activity will take the payment out of the ordinary course of business.").

199. *See* Marathon Oil Co. v. Flatau (*In re* Craig Oil Co.), 785 F.2d 1563, 1566 (11th Cir. 1986) (finding no error in lower court's consideration of debtor's motive for continued payment to Marathon).

200. *Id.*

201. Gull Air, Inc. v. Beech Acceptance Corp., Inc. (*In re* Gull Air, Inc.), 82 B.R. 1 (Bankr. D. Mass. 1988) (holding that transfers from debtor to creditor pursuant to the workout agreement were not consistent with the prior transactions between the parties and therefore rejecting creditor's ordinary course defense).

202. 5-547 *Collier on Bankruptcy* 547.04[2][a][ii] (16th ed. 2016) (stating that "the court will examine and compare the relationship between such collection activity and the making of the challenged payment with the pre-preference period relationship between collection activity and payment"); *see* Sparkman v. Martin Marietta Materials, Inc. (*In re* Mainline Contracting, Inc.), 68 C.B.C. 2d 736, 2012 Bankr. LEXIS 4986 (Bankr. E.D.N.C. 2012) (finding transfers were made in ordinary course of business between debtor and creditor because during the preference period, the defendant took the same measures to collect on accounts receivable that it took during the baseline period).

collection pressure never happened before or is otherwise not consistent with past conduct, you can probably forget proving an ordinary course defense. Ideally, you want to provide circumstantial evidence, in the form of a long history of collection pressure, that collection pressure in the preference period had nothing to do with the looming bankruptcy.[203]

Types of Collection Pressure

There's collection pressure, and then there's Collection Pressure.[204] The most common and most innocuous form is merely emails or telephone calls following up on an invoice.[205] It's likely that this low level of collection activity also happened in the base period.[206]

A more extreme form of collection pressure is threatening to hold back products or services unless the customer/debtor pays past invoices.[207] You see this type of collection pressure when the debtor has not paid for months or is unusually late. Since this extreme collection pressure often occurs right before bankruptcy, courts interpret this conduct as "Exhibit A" supporting the finding of an inexcusable preferential payment. Courts will view this behavior as the specific conduct preference laws are meant to discourage. The implication is that the creditor not only received preferential treatment but actively sought it to avoid the fate of other creditors. (bad intent).

---

203. *See* McCarthy v. Navistar Fin. Corp. (*In re* Vogel Van & Storage, Inc.), 210 B.R. 27 (N.D.N.Y. 1997) (finding payment was made in ordinary course of business because there was no evidence that calls from the creditor to the debtor contained economic or other coercion to induce unusual payment); *see also In re Craig Oil Co.*, 785 F.2d at 1566 ("[W]henever [a] bankruptcy court receives evidence of unusual collection efforts, it must consider whether the debtor's payment was in fact a response to those efforts.").

204. *See* 5-547 *Collier on Bankruptcy* 547.04[2][a][ii] (16th ed. 2016) ("The more intense the collection activity during the preference period the greater the likelihood that the activity will take the payment out of the ordinary course of business."); *see also* Writing Sales Ltd. Partnership v. Pilot Corp. of Am. (*In re* Writing Sales Ltd. Partnership), 96 B.R. 175, 179 (Bankr. E.D. Wis. 1989) (citing the intensity of pressure put on debtor to bring its account current and rejecting creditor's ordinary course of business defense).

205. *See* Grant v. Suntrust Bank, Central Florida, N.A. (*In re* L. Bee Furniture Co., Inc.), 203 B.R. 778 (Bankr. M.D. Fla. 1996) (accepting ordinary course defense because the creditor followed its routine collection activities, which included sending invoices, past due notices, and phone calls—these activities did not increase during the preference period).

206. Most evidence of collection pressure is found in emails. During discovery, the plaintiff will most likely demand all email correspondence that took place between the parties in search of collection pressure.

207. *See* Boone v. Marlatt (*In re* Day Telecommunications, Inc.), 70 B.R. 904 (Bankr. E.D.N.C. 1987) (rejecting ordinary course defense, and emphasizing that never before had the creditor refused to perform further services if he did not receive immediate assurance of payment, and never before had the defendant received payment so soon after submitting his bill).

However, even extreme collection pressure may be defensible.[208] It may be that this kind of pressure had been applied many times before. Sometimes a vendor may have routinely made threats for years.[209] A history of routine extreme collection pressure demonstrates that this conduct is unrelated to an imminent bankruptcy. A threatening creditor can still be an accidental preference recipient.

Another strategy is to argue that the extreme collection pressure did not affect how the debtor paid. As noted above, some courts agree that the collection pressure must have resulted in some actual non-ordinary debtor conduct to defeat the ordinary course defense.[210] In many courts, however, this argument may be a loser.

3.3.1.2.7.2 Change in the Form of Payment

If the debtor always paid by check during the base period and then suddenly switched to wires during the preference period, a court may consider this a critical factor in finding a lack of consistency and thus a lack of ordinariness in the preference period.[211]

Maybe the vendor arm-twisted the debtor to wire funds before a bankruptcy or before the money was spent paying other vendors. Perhaps a sudden wire implies that the vendor took an active role in getting preferred. The ordinary course defense is meant to protect accidental re-

---

208. *See* Branch v. Ropes & Gray (*In re* Bank of New England Corp.), 161 B.R. 557, 24 Bankr. Ct. Dec. (CRR) 1621 (Bankr. D. Mass. 1993) (rejecting trustee's argument that the creditor's collection practices in the form of heightened requests for payment meant that the debtor's payments were not made in the ordinary course of business in compliance with 11 U.S.C. § 547(c)(2)(B)).

209. *See In re L. Bee Furniture Co.*, 203 B.R. at 783 (allowing ordinary course of business defense, noting, "In this case, Defendant followed its routine collection activities. Defendant sent invoices to the Debtor prior to the due date, which were then followed by past due notices, followed by phone calls. These activities were routine over the life of the loan, and Defendant's collection activities did not increase during the preference period.").

210. *See* McCarthy v. Navistar Fin. Corp. (*In re* Vogel Van & Storage, Inc.), 210 B.R. 27 (N.D.N.Y. 1997) (finding payment was made in ordinary course of business because there was no evidence that calls from the creditor to the debtor contained economic or other coercion to induce unusual payment); *see also In re Craig Oil Co.*, 785 F.2d at 1566 ("[W]henever [a] bankruptcy court receives evidence of unusual collection efforts, it must consider whether the debtor's payment was in fact a response to those efforts.").

211. 5-547 *Collier on Bankruptcy* 547.04[2][a][ii] (16th ed. 2016) (stating that "if the transfer under scrutiny was by wire transfer or cashier's check, the transferee must show that this type of payment falls within the circle of ordinary course transactions between the parties"); *see also* Central Hardware Co. v. Sherwin-Williams Co. (*In re* Spirit Holding Co., Inc.), 153 F.3d 902 (8th Cir. 1998); Tomlins v. BRW Paper Co., Inc. (*In re* Tulsa Litho Co.), 229 B.R. 806 (B.A.P. 10th Cir. 1999); Modern Metal Prods. Co. v. Virtual Engineering, Inc. (*In re* Modern Metal Prods. Co.), 2015 Bankr. LEXIS 1188 (Bankr. N.D. Ill. 2015).

cipients, not intentional recipients. On the other hand, maybe the debtor had a long-range plan to switch to wire transfers that had nothing to do with collection pressure.[212]

As with collection pressure, some courts, applying a more mechanical interpretation, will find a change to wire to be in and of itself sufficient to knock out the ordinary course defense.

3.3.1.2.7.2.1 The Practical Skinny on Handling This Factor

Let's say you get a wire or overnight check, and you never got one before, and this happens in the preference period three days before a bankruptcy. As we have seen above, the implication will be that you were arm-twisting so you could get paid before the music stopped. You must rebut this circumstantial evidence by providing an alternative explanation. The plaintiff will argue that a change to wire is by itself non-ordinary.

However, if you can prove, for example, that the debtor's switch to payments by ACH was long planned and unrelated to the bankruptcy or collection pressure, you might be able to preserve your defense.

The plaintiff will argue the importance case law gives to consistency. You must argue that *in this special situation* inconsistency is irrelevant. A switch to ACH is no evidence that you engineered a payment at the expense of fellow vendors. Despite the change to a wire, you are still just another accidental preference recipient. If you were also paid in the same time frame as usual, that's more evidence of payment accidental-ness, i.e., lack of bad intent.

3.3.1.2.8 Payments on Account

A payment "on account" means a partial payment of one invoice or partial payment towards a group of invoices.[213] So for example, you send the debtor two invoices, one for $25,672.50 and the second in the amount of

---

212. *See In re AE Liquidation, Inc.*, 2013 Bankr. LEXIS 4144 at *16 (finding wire transfer was made voluntarily by debtor and not at the creditor's instance).

213. *See* Ames Merch. Corp. v. Cellmark Paper Inc. (Ames Dep't Stores, Inc.), 450 B.R. 24 (Bankr. S.D.N.Y. 2011) (rejecting ordinary course defense because "lump sum or partial payments" made by debtor were not consistent with the parties' payment scheme before preferential period).

$32,433.52. During the preference period, the debtor sends you a check for $30,000.

The implication is that the debtor is making a partial payment under pressure, to keep you at bay. If a lot of other creditors are not getting paid anything, the implication is also that the debtor intended to prefer you particularly.

The best defense, as usual, is to see if the debtor ever paid you on account in the past.[214] If the debtor always paid on account in the base period or at least did it regularly, it is likely that your payment on account "accidentally" coincided with the looming bankruptcy. The argument is that the past habit of on account payments contradicts the implication that the debtor suddenly acquired a prebankruptcy intent to prefer you or that you applied special pressure.

Ordinariness of the Transaction as a Whole

The Bankruptcy Code provides that not only does the payment need to be ordinary concerning the timeliness of past payments, it also needs to be the kind of payment that's ordinary for the debtor.[215]

Sometimes the trustee will use this provision to blow up an ordinary course defense even if the payment was on time or paid precisely in the same time frame like every other past payment. The concept is that the entire transaction was not ordinary for the debtor.

For example, let's say the debtor is in the business of selling fresh fish and pays you to Feng Shuai its offices. The trustee might argue that payments for Feng Shuai interior designing are unrelated to the fish business and thus non-ordinary.

The counterargument to that is that it is ordinary for businesses to spend money on office furnishings.

---

214. *See* PN Chapter 11 Estate Liquidating Trust v. Inserts East, Inc. (*In re* Philadelphia Newspapers, LLC), 468 B.R. 712 (Bankr. E.D. Pa. 2012) (featuring argument by defendant that "'the [h]istory between the parties establishes that payments were made [in lump sum] on account of multiple invoices' and that 'this was common practice between the parties'" (quoting Affidavit of defendant's CFO)).

215. 5-547 *Collier on Bankruptcy* 547[2][a][iii] (16th ed. 2016) (stating that "under section 547(c)(2)(B), even if the challenged payments were irregular, they may be considered 'ordinary' for purposes of section 547(c)(2) if they were consistent with the patterns within a relevant industry").

Another example is a business that pays a debt-restructuring consultant during the preference period. In an actual case, a trustee argued that debt restructuring was not central to the debtor's business and therefore a payment to a restructuring consultant could not be in the ordinary course. The court dismissed the trustee's argument, opining that it is ordinary for companies to hire debt restructuring people when they are in financial trouble.[216]

The trustee will very rarely argue this provision, but don't be blindsided.

3.3.1.3 Ordinary for the Industry

A second, alternative, way to prove an ordinary course defense is to show that the payments were ordinary for the industry. This defense is the so-called "industry standard" defense. You can use this argument as an alternative to proving that the payments were ordinary between the parties, or you can use both.

The concept behind the industry-standard defense is simple. If the payment during the preference period was ordinary for the relevant industry, then it's protected as being ordinary.[217] For example, let's say you try the ordinary-between-the-parties defense, and you run into problems. The debtor was paying every invoice in precisely 30 days and then suddenly during the preference period the debtor starts paying in 60 days.

The industry-standard defense provides that if the 60-day payment is ordinary for the industry, then these payments are protected from avoidance even though they varied from the parties' past conduct.[218]

---

216. See Lawson v. Ford Motor Co. (*In re* Roblin Indus., Inc.), 78 F.3d 30 (2d Cir. 1996) (ruling that a payment made pursuant to a debt restructuring agreement could be considered an ordinary business term if evidence is provided that it is within industry practice).

217. 5-547 *Collier on Bankruptcy* 547[2][a][iii] (16th ed. 2016) ("Courts have uniformly held that 'ordinary business terms' . . . implies an objective standard based on the relevant industry."); *see* Gulf City Seafoods, Inc. v. Ludwig Shrimp Co. (*In re* Gulf City Seafoods, Inc.), 296 F.3d 363 (5th Cir. 2002) ("[W]e compare the credit arrangements between other similarly situated debtors and creditors in the industry to see whether the payment practices at issue are consistent with what takes place in the industry.").

218. Willson v. McPhersons Partnership (*In re* Central Louisiana Grain Cooperative, Inc.), 497 B.R. 229 (Bankr. W.D. La. 2013) (noting that ordinary course of business defense cannot be satisfied by proof of creditor's own dealings with debtor—it requires reference to external data involving other creditors and debtors in the relevant industry).

The problem with the industry-standard defense is that it is difficult and expensive to prove.[219]

Let's say Moe paid Curly in 60 days during the preference period and before that he always paid in 30 days. Curly will probably need to show an industry standard defense to have any ordinary course defense at all.

Curly's first issue is deciding what industry is relevant.[220] Curly may choose to argue that the appropriate industry is the national carwashing industry. Moe might want to say that the industry is passenger car detailing. Whether to use the industry of the debtor or the vendor may not be a settled legal issue depending on the location of the court.[221]

Let's assume that a court determines that the relevant industry is passenger car detailing. Curly then needs to find the right kind of evidence for his assertion that most car detailers in the industry get paid in 60 days. Maybe he attended a seminar at a convention of car detailers about how long customers typically take to pay. Perhaps, he networked with other car dealers. Perhaps, Curly worked for several car detailers, and they all got paid in 60 days. Courts might accept evidence based on Curly's knowledge, but it will have to be detailed and convincing. However, many courts might see Curly's testimony as biased and self-serving, and so may give it less weight.[222]

Curly's other option is to hire an expert who can testify, based on the expert's experience in the car detailing business, that it's ordinary in the industry for vendors to get paid in 60 days.[223] The problem with hiring

---

219. *In re* Tolona Pizza Products Corp., 3 F.3d at 1033 ("Not only is it difficult to identify the industry whose norm shall govern . . . but there can be great variance in billing practices within an industry.").

220. 5-547 *Collier on Bankruptcy*, 547.04[2][a][iii] (16th ed. 2016) ("In order to determine whether the defendant has satisfied its burden of showing that the payments were within industry standards, the court must first define the relevant industry." (citing Lawson v. Ford Motor Co. (*In re* Roblin Indus., Inc.), 78 F.3d 30 (2d Cir. 1996))).

221. *See* Shodeen v. Airline Software, Inc. (*In re* Accessair, Inc.), 314 B.R. 386, 394 (B.A.P. 8th Cir. 2004) (holding it is the debtor's industry that is the focus of the "ordinary business terms" analysis); *see also* Advo-System, Inc. v. Maxway Corp., 37 F.3d 1044 (4th Cir. 1994) (holding that the industry standard to be applied when examining ordinary business terms is that of the creditor's industry).

222. 5-547 *Collier on Bankruptcy* 547.04[2][a][iii] (16th ed. 2016) ("Courts have given varying weight to testimony of an employee of the creditor depending on the extent of experience of the employee and the quality of the testimony.").

223. *Id.* ("Relevant evidence might include the testimony of disinterested experts not employed by the creditor and of an employee of the transferee[;] . . . the weight given to expert witnesses depends both on the credentials of the expert and the quality of the expert's testimony."); *see also* G.H. Leidenheimer Baking Co., Ltd. v. Sharp (*In re* SGSM Acquisition Co., LLC), 439 F.3d 233 (5th Cir. 2006) (holding that bankruptcy court did not err in holding that the defendants'

an expert is cost. Not only is the expert's initial review time expensive, but Curly will also have to pay for an expert report and for the expert to testify at depositions and trial.

Also, the plaintiff trustee will hire his own expert on the car detailing business. The trustee's expert may well testify that the industry standard is 30 days, not 60 days. A lot of litigation and cost, and in the end, it comes down to which of the battling experts to believe and little basis for choosing that's better than a coin flip.

3.3.1.3.1 Practical Tips on the Industry Standard

The Risk Management Association tracks the days outstanding that is typical for each industry.[224] If the report shows that you got paid right on target with the industry, you might be able to present a robust industry-standard defense.[225] At the very least, you should be able to get some leverage in negotiating with the plaintiff.

3.3.2 The Subsequent New Value Defense[226]

After ordinary course, the next defense we look at is the subsequent new value defense.[227] The fundamental principle of this defense is that if you shipped product or provided services *after* you received a preferential transfer, and you were *not paid*, you can set off the value of those products or services against the prior preferential transfer.[228]

---

witnesses failed to qualify as expert witnesses and thus the only evidence on the objective prong was the testimony of the plaintiff's expert witness).

224. *See* Simon v. Gerdau MacSteel, Inc. (*In re* Camshaft Specialties, Inc.), 444 B.R. 347 (Bankr. E.D. Mich. 2011) (featuring trustee's expert who relied on information from a Risk Management Association Report); *see also* Lightfoot v. Amelia Maritime Servs., Inc. (*In re* Sea Bridge Marine, Inc.), 412 B.R. 868 (Bankr. E.D. La. 2008) (featuring supplier's expert witness who used Risk Management Association report in her testimony regarding industry standard in the ordinary course of business defense).

225. *See* Simon v. Gerdau MacSteel, Inc. (*In re* American Camshaft Specialties, Inc.), 444 B.R. 347 (Bankr. E.D. Mich. 2011) (accepting ordinary course defense and concluding payments were in accordance with iron and steel mill industry standards after reviewing Risk Management Association report).

226. *See* 11 U.S.C. § 547(c)(4) ("The trustee may not avoid under this section a transfer . . . to or for the benefit of a creditor, to the extent that, after such transfer, such creditor gave new value to or for the benefit of the debtor—(A) not secured by an otherwise unavoidable security interest; and (B) on account of which new value the debtor did not make an otherwise unavoidable transfer to or for the benefit of such creditor[.]").

227. *See id.*

228. Harris P. Quinn, *The Subsequent New Value Exception Under Section 547(c)(4) of the Bankruptcy Code—Judicial*

The rationale for this defense is that it encourages folks to give unsecured credit to troubled companies.[229] A second rationale is that the debtor got to keep your stuff for free, so it seems fair to wipe out the requirement that you return the preference payment. Your unpaid-for shipment of goods is treated as equivalent to paying back the preference. So instead of paying back the preference with cash, you are deemed to have already paid it by your transfer of unpaid-for product or services.

You need to remember two important things about the subsequent new value defense. First, in most cases, you must have shipped product or rendered services and not have gotten paid for that product or services for it to count as "new value."[230]

Second, you must have shipped this product or rendered services *after* you received the alleged preferential payment.[231] That's why the Code calls it the *subsequent* new value defense.

Third, you can only wipe out the prior preferential payment to the extent of the value of your product or services.[232] For example, if you received a preferential payment of $10,000, and you shipped and were not paid for merchandise or services worth only $5,000, you can just reduce the preferential payment by $5,000. If there are no other defenses, you will

---

Gloss is Creditors' Loss, 24 Mem. St. U. L. Rev. 667, 675 (1994) (citing *In re* Thomas W. Garland, Inc., 19 B.R. 920 (Bankr. E.D. Mo. 1982) (prescribing the method by which subsequent new value should be applied: "'each dollar of preferential payment may be set off against each dollar of the following subsequent advances . . .'" (quoting *In re* M & L Business Mach. Co., Inc., 160 B.R. 851, 855 (Bankr. D. Colo. 1993))); Vern Countryman, *Bankruptcy Preferences—Current Law and Proposed Changes*, 11 U.C.C. L.J. 95, 103 (1978) (stating that "even though a creditor has received a preference . . . the creditor may still offset any subsequent unsecured credit which was extended to the debtor").

229. 5-547 *Collier on Bankruptcy* 547.04[4][a] (16th ed. 2016) ("The exception of section 547(c)(4) is intended to encourage creditors to work with troubled companies and to remove the unfairness of allowing the trustee to void all transfers made by the debtor to a creditor during the preference period without giving any corresponding credit for subsequent advances of new value to the debtor for which the preference defendant was not paid." (citing Jones Truck Lines, Inc. v. Full Serv. Leasing Corp., 83 F.3d 253, 257 n.3 (8th Cir. 1996))).

230. *See* Pettigrew v. Trust Co. Bank (*In re* Bishop), 17 B.R. 180, 183 (1982) (interpreting § 547(c)(4)(B) as requiring new value to remain unpaid).

231. 5-547 *Collier on Bankruptcy*, 547.04[4] (16th ed. 2016) ("To 'the extent' that the transferee gives 'new value to or for the benefit of the debtor' on an unsecured basis after receiving a preferential transfer, the otherwise preferential payment will not be voidable . . . .").

232. Nick Sears, *Defeating the Preference System: Using the Subsequent New Value Defense and Administrative Expense Claims to "Double Dip,"* 28 Emory Bankr. Dev. J. 593, 599 (2012) ("When the estate of the debtor approaches the creditor to force the creditor to disgorge the preference under § 547(b), the creditor asserts that the goods shipped to the debtor after his preferential transfer offset the loss of value to the debtor's estate caused by the purported preferential transfer. Thus, the net value of the debtor's estate remained unchanged during the preference period."

still need to return the $5,000 part of the preferential transfer that was not set off by the value of your unpaid-for products or services.

3.3.2.1 Problems that Come Up

Sometimes the trustee will argue that the debtor never actually used any of your unpaid-for product or services. The concept of new value is that you essentially donated "new value" in the form of free products or services to the debtor. If the debtor never uses it, the trustee is going to argue: "Well, we got it for free, but we never used it and therefore got no value from it."[233] For example, if the debtor leased your warehouse and then stopped paying rent, you will argue that the ability to stay in the warehouse as a tenant is new value. The trustee may argue that the debtor moved out of the warehouse months before and the theoretical ability to use the warehouse was of no value to the debtor. This argument is relatively rare but don't be blindsided.

3.3.3 The Contemporaneous Exchange Defense[234]

This defense[235] exempts creditors from clawback of payments that did not involve the extension of credit. The theory is that the preference laws are designed to reverse preferential payments of *debts*. If no credit has been extended because the payment was made contemporaneously[236] upon receipt of goods or services, then no debt was ever created.

---

233. *See* Excel Enterprises, Inc. v. Sikes, Gardes & Co. (*In re* Excel Enterprises, Inc.), 83 B.R. 427, 431 (Bankr. W.D. La. 1988) (stating that new value involving the provision of services is deemed given on the date the personal services are rendered); *see also* Rushton v. E & S Int'l Enters., Inc. (*In re* Eleva, Inc.), 235 B.R. 486, 489-90 (B.A.P. 10th Cir. 1999) (stating that creditor extends new value at the time the goods are shipped).

234. *See* 11 U.S.C. § 547(c)(1) ("The trustee may not avoid under this section a transfer . . . to the extent that such transfer was—(A) intended by the debtor and the creditor to or for whose benefit such transfer was made to be a contemporaneous exchange for new value given to the debtor; and (B) in fact a substantially contemporaneous exchange[.]").

235. *See* Velde v. Kirsch, 543 F.3d 469, 472 (8th Cir. 2008) (stating that the purpose of the contemporaneous exchange exception is to protect transactions that do not result in a diminution of the bankruptcy estate).

236. See Silverman Consulting, Inc. v. Canfor Wood Prods. Mktg. (*In re* Payless Cashways, Inc.), 306 B.R. 243 (B.A.P. 8th Cir. 2004) (finding that where a bankruptcy debtor agreed to pay for lumber upon delivery under a destination contract, the debtor's payments upon or before delivery constituted contemporaneous exchanges for new value rather than avoidable preferential transfers); see also Suhar v. Agree Auto Servs., Inc. (*In re* Blakely), 497 B.R. 267 (Bankr. N.D. Ohio 2013) (holding that creditor could not avail itself of the contemporaneous exchange for new value defense because the debtor's payment was applied to the amount due and owing on a trade-in vehicle, not toward the purchase of a new vehicle).

For example, the debtor bought bananas from your store. He paid immediately for the bananas, and you contemporaneously handed him a bag of bananas. Even if the debtor paid you and no other creditors, no unfairness would result. It's not unfair because he is not paying money he "owes." He is not favoring you over others to whom he owes money. He's just exchanging money for "new value" (bananas). If he paid an old debt to you, he would not be getting anything back in the form of new value.

This defense requires you to prove two elements. The first element is that the exchange was "contemporaneous." The second element is that both parties intended[237] a contemporaneous exchange.[238]

Courts vary in their rulings about what "contemporaneous" means.[239]

Some bankruptcy judges have permitted a time gap[240] of 14 days between delivery of product and receipt of payment to be a "contemporaneous" exchange. Typically, the less time that has elapsed between the transfer of the product or service and payment, the more likely it is that a court will allow the contemporaneous exchange defense.

The second element is harder to prove. It's easy to prove your own intent just by saying what your intent was. It's hard as heck to prove somebody else's intent. The entire body of preference laws was revised based on the difficulty of establishing what's in somebody's mind. Some bankruptcy courts have accepted circumstantial evidence to prove debtor intent. For

---

237. *See* Grogan v. Southwest Textiles, Inc. (*In re* Advance Glove Mfg. Co.), 42 B.R. 489, 493 (Bankr. E.D. Mich. 1984) (stating that agreement between parties can evidence contemporaneous intent); Pfau v. First Nat'l Bank (*In re* Schmidt), 26 B.R. 89, 91 (Bankr. D. Minn. 1982) (stating that course of dealing between parties can show contemporaneous intent); *see also* Post-Confirmation Comm. v. Tomball Forest, Ltd. (*In re* Bison Bldg. Holdings, Inc.), 473 B.R. 168 (Bankr. S.D. Tex. 2012) (finding that the evidence showed that the debtor regularly paid the creditor one month after issuance of invoices; thus, the parties intended that the exchanges not be contemporaneous).

238. *See Velde*, 543 F.3d at 472 (stating that if new value is given, a contemporaneous exchange does not diminish the estate).

239. *See* Pine Top Ins. Co. v. Bank of Am. Nat'l Trust & Savs. Assoc., 969 F.2d 321, 328 (7th Cir. 1992) (stating that contemporaneousness is a flexible concept that requires a case-by-case inquiry into all relevant circumstances—such as length of delay, reason for delay, nature of the transaction, intentions of the parties, and possible risk of fraud—surrounding an allegedly preferential transfer).

240. *See* Dill v. Brad Hall & Assocs., Inc. (*In re* Indian Capitol Distrib.), No. 7-09-11558 SA, 2012 Bankr. LEXIS 3725 (Bankr. D. N.M. 2012) (holding that although payments by bankruptcy debtor to transferee were preferential transfers, transfers were not avoidable under 11 U.S.C. § 547(c) since payments on or about 10 days after fuel was delivered to debtor was substantially contemporaneous exchange for value).

example, if someone picked out some bananas and then handed you five dollars, it's clear from the circumstances that the banana buyer intended to enter into a contemporaneous exchange with you. You don't need to depose him.

However, you should not assume that this will always be the case. You may need to depose the debtor or otherwise find evidence that proves that the debtor had the intent[241] to enter into a contemporaneous exchange with you.

---

241. "The critical inquiry in determining whether there has been a contemporaneous exchange for new value is whether the parties intended such an exchange." McClendon v. Cal-Wood Door (In re Wadsworth Bldg. Components, Inc.), 711 F.2d 122, 124 (9th Cir. 1983). Courts determine the parties' intent by examining evidence of the parties' mutual understanding of the payment arrangement and evidence of how payments were reflected on the parties' books. See Hechinger Inv. Co. of Del., Inc. v. Universal Forest Prods., Inc. (In re Hechinger Inv. Co. of Delaware, Inc.), 489 F.3d 568, 575 (3d Cir. 2007) (holding that the existence of a credit relationship does not preclude a finding that a contemporaneous exchange was intended and noting that the parties had a general understanding that payments would be made at essentially the same time shipments were received) (citing Silverman Consulting, Inc. v. Canfor Wood Prods. Mktg. (In re Payless Cashways, Inc.), 306 B.R. 243, 247-54 (8th Cir. BAP 2004)); Barnes v. Karbank Holdings, LLC (In re JS & RB, Inc.), 446 B.R. 350, 357 (Bankr. W.D. Mo. 2011) (finding that a contemporaneous exchange was intended when the payment was equal to the amount owed for monthly rent).

Bankruptcy Preference Clawbacks in Plain English

CHAPTER 4

The Players

It can be beneficial to know who will play what roles during your case.

4.1   The Judge

The Bankruptcy Code controls everything that happens throughout the bankruptcy case.[242] The Code is like the blueprint for building a house. The entire process (and every possible detail about the process) is set out in rules found in the Bankruptcy Code.[243] The problem is, lawyers being lawyers, they debate the exact meaning of every rule. The first job of the bankruptcy judge is to resolve arguments about how he should interpret these rules.[244]

The second role of the bankruptcy judge is to make sure the rules are followed.

The third job of the bankruptcy judge is to set schedules so that an

---

242. *See* Rafael I. Pardo and Kathryn A. Watts, *The Structural Exceptionalism of Bankruptcy Administration*, 60 UCLA L. Rev. 384, 408 (2012) (stating that "the Bankruptcy Code efficiently effectuates the shift to a compulsory and collective proceeding").

243. For the sake of simplicity I treat the Bankruptcy Code as including the Federal Rules of Bankruptcy Procedure, Local Bankruptcy Rules and any other rules that govern a case.

244. Alan M. Ahart, *The Limited Scope of Implied Powers of a Bankruptcy Judge: A Statutory Court of Bankruptcy, Not a Court of Equity*, 79 Am. Bankr. L.J. 1, 9 (2005) (stating that "the task of a bankruptcy judge is to interpret the Bankruptcy Code").

individual or company in bankruptcy is moved through the process promptly.[245]

The fourth role of the bankruptcy judge is to resolve disputes in the same way that a trial judge decides disputes.[246]

There are a few important things to remember about the bankruptcy judge:

- It's not his role to judge the unfairness or fairness of the preference laws. Write to your congressional representative.

- He generally will not respond to letters and should not communicate with any party privately.

- He does not generally meet with the parties privately, and it's not his job to resolve disputes informally.

The job of the bankruptcy judge is to apply the law as drafted by Congress.[247] You may think (correctly) that the preference laws are unfair, but complaining to the bankruptcy judge will be ineffective. The only way to have an impact is to write your congressman (and send him a copy of this book).

Judges are not supposed to communicate privately with the parties[248] because it's unfair for one side to present arguments in the absence of another party. There is a process in place for making arguments and being heard by the judge. The rules provide for hearings and the filing

---

245. Harvey R. Miller, *The Changing Face of Chapter 11: A Reemergence of the Bankruptcy Judge as Producer, Director, and Sometimes Star of the Reorganization Passion Play*, 69 Am. Bankr. L.J. 431, 439 (1995) (stating that the role of a bankruptcy judge is "to ensure that the case is handled expeditiously and economically" by "(i) setting a date by which the debtor must assume or reject an executory contract or unexpired lease; (ii) setting a date by which the debtor must file a disclosure statement and plan; (iii) setting the date by which a party in interest other than a debtor may file a plan; (iv) setting a date by which a proponent of a plan, other than the debtor, shall solicit acceptances of such plan; (v) fixing the scope and format of the notice regarding the hearing to approve a disclosure statement; and (vi) providing that such hearing may be combined with the hearing on confirmation of a plan"); *see also* 11 U.S.C. § 105(d).

246. United Student Aid Funds, Inc. v. Espinosa, 559 U.S. 260, 277 (2010) ("[T]he Code makes plain that bankruptcy courts have the authority—indeed, the obligation—to direct a debtor to conform his plan to the requirements" of the Bankruptcy Code).

247. *Id.*

248. Fed. R. Bankr. P. 9003(a) ("Except as otherwise permitted by applicable law, any examiner, any party in interest, and any attorney, accountant, or employee of a party in interest shall refrain from ex parte meetings and communications with the court concerning matters affecting a particular case or proceeding.").

of legal briefs.[249] If you can't find a lawyer to defend you and you want to defend yourself, you're going to have to learn and pay attention to the rules like everybody else.

Judges don't sit in on mediation sessions.[250] This is for the excellent and obvious reason that you want people to relax during mediation and not worry about making an impression on the judge who can decide your case. In bankruptcy, mediation is conducted by a mediator. Unlike some non-bankruptcy settlement processes, the bankruptcy mediator does not issue a decision, and mediation is not binding.[251]

4.1.1 What Makes Judges Happy

I am, of course, speculating but I suspect that Judges like to see creditors get paid.[252] The primary purpose of corporate bankruptcy is to keep businesses alive, to save jobs and get creditors paid.[253] If reorganization accomplishes these goals, the judge, I would expect, is going to feel like she's providing a valuable service to the community. If the business dies and creditors get paid very little, that's probably much less rewarding for a bankruptcy judge.

Assuming the judge believes in the rationales for the preference claw-back laws, she will be happy if unsecured creditors are paid significantly more because funds were clawed back into the estate.

---

249. *See* Fed. R. Bankr. P. 9014(a) ("In a contested matter not otherwise governed by these rules, relief shall be requested by motion, and reasonable notice and opportunity for hearing shall be afforded the party against whom relief is sought.").

250. Miller, *supra* note 247, at 437 ("Several bankruptcy judges have used outside third parties in order to resolve claims disputes or develop a consensus regarding a plan through mediation."); for an example of a successful mediation effort involving a third-party mediator, not the bankruptcy judge, see *In re* R.H. Macy & Co., Nos. 92 B 40477-40486 (Bankr. S.D.N.Y. 1994).

251. Miller, *supra* note 247, at 436 ("Mediation, as currently used in certain districts, is a nonbinding process that introduces an impartial person to induce rationality among the parties and avoid expensive, vexatious, and protracted pursuit of litigation tactics or stalemated negotiations.").

252. *Id.* (citing 140 Cong. Rec. S14,464 (daily ed. Oct. 6, 1994) (statement of Sen. Brown)) (Chapter 11 reorganization is supposed to be about "allowing an otherwise viable business to quantify, consolidate, and manage its debt so that it can satisfy its creditors to the maximum extent feasible, but without threatening its continued existence and the thousands of jobs it provides.").

253. *Id.*

4.2   The Trustee

The trustee is not your enemy. I know a lot of trustees, and they're pretty nice guys and gals. Generally, trustees are bankruptcy lawyers who for some reason wanted to be trustees, so they applied to get on a "panel" of trustees. The trustee's job is to maximize the value of the bankruptcy estate.[254] He is *required* to pursue clawback claims that will bring money into the estate at a reasonable cost.[255] In fact, if he does not pursue clawback claims, and should have, he could be deemed negligent and held liable.[256]

In a Chapter 7 liquidation case, where a company is no longer a going concern, the court will usually appoint a trustee.[257] Courts also sometimes appoint trustees as part of a Chapter 11 plan if the plan sets up a trust for creditors.[258]

The trustee will usually hire a law firm to pursue clawbacks and other forms of litigation.[259] However, the trustee, as the "client," has the final say, generally speaking, in settlement negotiations.

---

254. Nancy L. Sanborn, Note: *Avoidance Recoveries in Bankruptcy: For the Benefit of the Estate or the Secured Creditor?* 90 Colum. L. Rev. 1376, 1377 (1990) ("Avoidance recoveries generally are considered to be available for all administrative and unsecured claimants and interest holders based on the Code's requirements that the trustee recovers transfers and preserves liens 'for the benefit of the estate.'").

255. *Id.* at 1389 ("A principal duty of the trustee in bankruptcy is to gather the assets of the estate; the grant of power to recover improper transfers is an important component of the associated duty to maximize the value of the estate.").

256. Daniel B. Bogart, *Finding the Still Small Voice: The Liability of Bankruptcy Trustees and the Work of the National Bankruptcy Review Commission*, 102 Dick. L. Rev. 703 (1998) ("Trustees are held to standards of care ranging from personal liability for negligence to personal liability for willful and intentional acts in violation of the trustee's duties.").

257. *See* Springel v. Prosser (*In re* Prosser), 2009 Bankr. LEXIS 3209 (Bankr. D. V.I. 2009) (directing the UST to immediately appoint a Chapter 7 trustee); *see also* Elizabeth H. McCullough, *Bankruptcy Trustee Liability: Is There a Method in the Madness?* 15 Lewis & Clark L. Rev. 153, 160 (2011) ("Chapter 7 trustees are charged specifically with the additional obligations of collecting and reducing to money property of the debtor's estates and closing the estates as expeditiously as possible.").

258. *See* John Mitchell, Inc. v. Steinbrugge (*In re* Hanna), 72 F.3d 114 (9th Cir. 1995) (featuring appointment of trustee in Chapter 11 case after the filing of the petitioner for reorganization by the Chapter 11 debtor); *see also* McCullough, *supra* note 259, at 160 ("Chapter 11 trustees . . . are charged specifically with the duties of investigating fully the debtors and their businesses, filing plans of reorganization, and unless courts order otherwise, operating the debtors' businesses.").

259. *See* Spencer D. Solomon, *Bankruptcy Best Practices from the Bench and Bar: Keeping Things In-House: Increasing Scrutiny of the Chapter 7 Trustee's Selection of Counsel*, 55 S. Tex. L. Rev. 665 (2014) (discussing the statutory and ethical standards courts must consider when a trustee wants to hire his own counsel); *see also* 11 U.S.C. § 327(a) ("Employment of professional persons").

Trustees are typically paid a portion of the assets they are able to recover for the estate.[260]

4.3   The Creditors' Committee

The creditors' committee is composed of the 20 largest unsecured creditors.[261] Sometimes the creditors' committee will file clawback suits[262] on the theory that bringing money back into the bankruptcy estate from a few unsecured creditors who got special treatment will benefit all unsecured creditors.[263] (Of course, if *all or most* unsecured creditors are sued for preferences (often the case), this rationale is unavailable.) Typically, though, trustees or debtor counsel will bring clawback actions.[264] Regardless of who brings the actions, the creditors' committee typically retains an attorney to represent it in clawback actions and/or the bankruptcy generally.[265]

4.4   The Debtor

The debtor is the entity that filed for bankruptcy, either voluntarily or not.[266] For simplicity's sake, this handbook focuses on business, gener-

---

260. *See* 11 U.S.C. § 326(a); Mohns, Inc. v. Lanser, 522 B.R. 594 (Bankr. E.D. Wis. 2015).

261. *See* 11 U.S.C. § 1102 ("Creditors' and equity security holders' committees"); *see also* Klee & Shaffer, *supra* note 2, at 1003 (stating that "the U.S. Trustee typically makes its committee selections from a list of the twenty largest creditors filed by the debtor at or near the commencement of the case pursuant to Rule 1007(d) of the Federal Rules of Bankruptcy Procedure").

262. 5-547 *Collier on Bankruptcy* 547.11[6] (16th ed. 2016) (stating that "most lower courts today recognize the concept of derivative standing and will allow a creditors' committee or other party in interest to initiate and prosecute a preference or other avoidance action on behalf of the estate"); *see also* Canadian Pac. Forest Prods. Ltd. v. J.D. Irving, Ltd. (*In re* Gibson Group, Inc.), 66 F.3d 1436, 1446 (6th Cir. 1995) (setting forth detailed steps that must be followed before creditor or creditors' committee can obtain derivative standing to bring avoidance action on behalf of the estate); Official Unsecured Creditors Committee of Sufolla, Inc. v. U.S. Nat'l Bank of Oregon (*In re* Sufolla, Inc.), 2 F.3d 977, 979 n.1 (9th Cir. 1993) (stating committee may obtain derivative standing to bring preference action when trustee or Chapter 11 debtor unjustifiably fails to do so).

263. Klee & Shaffer, *supra* note 2, at 1041 (stating that a creditors committee's principal tasks include "protecting and promoting the interests of its constituents and attempting to maximize any recoveries from the estate for them").

264. *Id.* at 1040 (stating that "the authority of debtors-in-possession under section 1107 to carry out nearly all of the powers and duties of a trustee significantly tempers the committee's role in carrying out actions on behalf of the estate").

265. *Id.* ("An official creditors' committee . . . may employ one or more attorneys, accountants, or other professionals at the expense of the estate."); *see also* 11 U.S.C. § 1103(a).

266. *See* 11 U.S.C. § 109.

ally corporate, debtors. In a Chapter 7 case, the trustee takes charge of the debtor and manages the case.[267] In a Chapter 11 case, on the other hand, the debtor's management generally stays in control.[268] In Chapter 11, the debtor will propose a plan of reorganization that typically has a provision in it for preference and fraudulent conveyance clawback litigation.[269] Sometimes the plan will create a trust to pursue clawbacks and appoint a trustee to handle clawback litigation.[270]

4.5   The Lawyers

The bankruptcy process is managed, run, and argued about by lawyers.[271] If you go to a hearing in bankruptcy court in a big case, such as the General Motors bankruptcy, it looks like an American Bar Association convention.

When you get sued for a clawback, the case is going to be prepared by a lawyer, and a lawyer is typically going to make the decision on settlement or, most of the time, make a recommendation to another lawyer, i.e., the trustee, who will then get the settlement approved by another lawyer, the judge. Of course, your lawyer, who will often act in conjunction with your general corporate lawyer, will negotiate your case. A publisher who went through the Chapter 11 bankruptcy process called his book "A Feast for Lawyers."[272] Some eat better than others at this feast, but it's a pretty accurate title.

---

267. *See* 11 U.S.C. § 704.

268. Steve H. Nickles, *Behavioral Effect of New Bankruptcy Law on Management and Lawyers: Collage of Recent Statutes and Cases Discouraging Chapter 11 Bankruptcy*, 59 Ark. L. Rev. 329, 379 (2006) ("Ordinarily, a trustee is not appointed in a Chapter 11 case. The debtor in possession ("DIP") remains in control of or as the debtor, and the DIP enjoys all of the rights, powers, and duties of a trustee, including the rights to continue operating the business and exclusively control, in the beginning, formation of a plan of reorganization. The DIP is essentially the firm's management, and this management is typically constituted of the same people who controlled the firm before bankruptcy.").

269. *Id.*; *see also* 11 U.S.C. § 1121.

270. George J. Bachrach & Cynthia E. Rodgers-Waire, *The Surety's Rights to the Contract Funds in the Principal's Chapter 11 Bankruptcy Case*, 35 Tort & Ins. L.J. 1, 5 (1999) ("The trust may be an express trust, a statutory trust, or a constructive trust over property held by the Trustee or the Debtor."); *see also* Mid-Atlantic Supply, Inc. of Va. v. Three Rivers Aluminum Co. (*In re* Mid Atlantic Supply Co.), 790 F.2d 1121 (4th Cir. 1986); American States Inc. Co. v. Glover Constr. Co. (*In re* Glover Constr. Co., Inc.), 30 B.R. 873 (Bankr. W.D. Ky. 1983).

271. *See* Nancy B. Rapoport, *Seeing the Forest* and *the Trees: The Proper Role of the Bankruptcy Attorney*, 70 Ind. L.J. 783 (1995).

272. *See* Sol Stein, *Bankruptcy: A Feast for Lawyers* (M. Evans ed., 1992).

Different lawyers have different litigation styles and, depending partly on their fee arrangement with their client, different motivations.[273] Knowing what makes the plaintiff's lawyer tick can make the difference between settling for more than you should and saving thousands or tens of thousands of dollars.

4.5.1 Plaintiff's Lawyer's Motivation 101

The plaintiff's lawyer is working for a client, usually the trustee. The trustee can hire any law firm he wants.[274] Handling cases for a trustee is a significant competitive win for whatever law firm gets the business. A trustee is like an annuity for the firm because of her steady flow of cases.[275] It's the kind of stable, lucrative work that lawyers yearn for.[276]

4.5.2 Aggression Is Rewarded

To continue receiving new case assignments, these lawyers need to bring funds into bankruptcy estates by aggressively pursuing clawback cases. By doing that, they make the trustees who retain them happy because trustees are paid on a contingency basis.[277] As noted above, bringing money into the estate probably also make the judge happy because it increases the return to creditors.[278]

---

273. Rapoport, *supra* note 273, at 827 ("The various roles of bankruptcy lawyers shift both between issues and within issues: bankruptcy lawyers litigate; they draft business plans and documents; they negotiate in hallways and on the telephone; they wheedle and cajole and mollify. And they do many of these things simultaneously, all with their clients' interests in mind. Foremost among the tasks that bankruptcy lawyers perform is that of balancing the many interests that a bankruptcy case implicates.").

274. *See* 11 U.S.C. § 327(a); *see also* Solomon, *supra* note 261, at 699 (stating that "bankruptcy courts have recognized that 'as is true for any client, a trustee has wide latitude in selecting the legal counsel he wishes to employ' because 'the right to choose one's attorney stems from the confidentiality of the attorney-client relationship and the position of trust held by one's counsel'" (quoting *In re* Gem Tire & Serv. Co., 117 B.R. 874, 876 (Bankr. S.D. Tex. 1990))).

275. Solomon, *supra* note 261, at 677 (stating that "there is no question that representation of the Chapter 7 trustee can be lucrative").

276. *Id.*

277. *See* 11 U.S.C. § 326(a); Mohns, Inc. v. Lanser, 522 B.R. 594 (Bankr. E.D. Wis. 2015).

278. *Id.* at 670 (stating that an attorney working for the trustee and the creditor's interests "are generally aligned because the attorney does not receive compensation unless he or she succeeds in enlarging the estate").

4.5.3 Keep Those Meters Running

I think it makes a significant difference whether the plaintiff's lawyer is being paid by the hour or on a contingency basis.[279]

If the lawyer is working on an hourly basis, she has zero motivation to settle the case as quickly as possible.[280] In fact, the motivation is the opposite, since law firms make money by billing. The only time this is not true is in small cases: a lawyer would have a tough time justifying to the trustee or the bankruptcy judge a $25,000 fee for winning a $15,000 lawsuit.

Also, lawyers for the trustee must have their fees approved by the bankruptcy judge.[281] Interestingly, defendants seldom object to the fees that lawyers run up suing them, even though those costs reduce the assets of the estate in which defendants share.

4.5.4 She (Doesn't) Work Hard for the Money

I much prefer to deal with lawyers who are being paid on a contingency basis. These folks, unless they're irrational, must weigh the burden of work the law firm will have to do with the potential amount of money that will be paid in settlement or judgment.[282]

These lawyers typically are not enthusiastic about racking up hours. Since they are not being paid by the hour, their motivation is to work as little as possible and get paid as much as possible. For that reason, they tend to fold more quickly if the defendant puts up reasonable resistance.

---

279. *Id.* (stating that "an attorney working under a contingency fee arrangement is only entitled to compensation commensurate with her success in the appointed task . . . [while] an attorney employed by the Chapter 7 trustee on an hourly basis may be entitled to compensation regardless of whether he or she succeeds in enlarging the estate's assets").

280. *Id.*

281. *Id.* at 669 ("In addition to needing court approval for their employment, the trustee's lawyers must also seek approval of their fees by filing an application with the court detailing the services performed."); *see also* 11 U.S.C. § 328(a).

282. Nancy B. Rapoport, *The Case for Value Billing in Chapter 11*, 7 J. Bus. & Tech. L. 117, n.132 (2011) ("The advantage of a hybrid fixed/contingency fee is that it takes the 'must bill hours' pressure out of the equation, thus creating more incentives to work efficiently (the fixed fee part) and diligently (the contingency fee part)." (citing Robert E. Litan & Steven C. Salop, *Reforming the Lawyer-Client Relationship Through Alternative Billing Methods*, 77 Judicature 191, 194-97 (1994))).

4.5.5   Lawyer Types

Besides the different attitudes of a lawyer being paid by the hour and a lawyer being paid on contingency, various personalities come into play.

These are the kinds of plaintiffs' lawyers that I've come across:

- *The brawler.* This type of lawyer tends to view lawyer-to-lawyer relationships as a "clash of swords." This is the worst lawyer to have on the other side because, due to a chemical imbalance, she enjoys constant confrontation. The best strategy is to stay out of her sandbox and disengage. She will dismiss your case out of boredom and look elsewhere for her adrenalin rush.

- *The nitpicker.* This kind of lawyer is not hard to spot. He will point out insignificant typos in your correspondence. He will be punctilious about deadlines and refuse to grant extensions. The best strategy is just to ignore his time-wasting nonsense.

- *The seasoned negotiator.* This kind of lawyer is usually very experienced in litigation and doesn't waste a lot of time with posturing and picayune issues. She takes a realistic look at the strength of both sides' evidence and arguments and picks a number that makes sense. You want this kind of lawyer on the other side.

- *The secret brawler.* The secret brawler acts like the negotiator but really is interested in getting every advantage. With her, you'll think the case is going to be dismissed shortly and somehow months and then years go by with nothing being resolved. This kind of lawyer is a snake in the grass. She will wait until late afternoon on Friday to send threatening emails with the specific intent of ruining your weekend. Got a nasty email at 4:00 p.m. on December 24th? It must be the secret brawler.

CHAPTER 5

The Timeline

Most preference clawback cases are predictable. They follow the same pattern as most lawsuits. This is what's going to happen in your case, in chronological order:

- The plaintiff's lawyer files and serves a complaint[283] on you.

- You file and serve an answer.[284]

- The court schedules the first "pretrial"/status conference.

- The plaintiff's lawyer and your lawyer participate in a compulsory Rule 26(f) conference, which results in a proposed scheduling order that may be approved by the judge.

- The scheduling order sets dates for

  - the beginning of discovery and close of discovery,[285]

  - the beginning and close of mediation if required,

---

283. "The original or initial pleading by which an action is commenced under codes or Rules of Civil Procedure." *Black's Law Dictionary* 285 (6th ed. 1990).

284. "The response of a defendant to the plaintiff's complaint, denying in part or in whole the allegations made by the plaintiff." *Id.* at 91.

285. The word "discovery" refers to "the pre-trial devices that can be used by one party to obtain facts and information about the case from the other party in order to assist the party's preparation for trial," including but not limited to depositions, interrogatories, requests for production of documents or things. *Id.* at 466.

      o   the deadline for filing "dispositive" motions,

      o   a trial date, and

      o   other stuff.

- Both sides serve discovery demands.

- Both sides serve discovery responses.

- Mediation occurs.

- Negotiations take place.

- There may be a settlement, with a settlement stipulation executed by both sides and a motion for approval filed with the court.

- If the case is not settled, pretrial motions will be filed.

- A trial will take place.

- Post-trial briefs will be filed.

5.1   Plaintiff's Lawyer Files and Serves a Complaint[286]

Bankruptcy is unusual in that the plaintiff's lawyer does not have to serve you by personal service or certified mail. If the complaint gets lost in the regular U.S. mail, that's too bad. A default judgment will be entered against you.

Complaints filed in preference clawback cases are generally very boilerplate. There is some controversy about whether the plaintiff should research whether there are defenses or not. Pretty much, that issue has been resolved in favor of plaintiffs. Plaintiffs can file a bare-bones complaint in a preference case and not worry about whether you have ironclad defenses or no defenses. It's usually not their problem.[287]

---

286. *See* Fed. R. Bankr. P. 7004 ("Process; Service of Summons, Complaint").

287. *See* Fed. R. Bankr. P. 7008 ("General Rules of Pleading").

5.2 Defendant Files an Answer[288]

Most answers are what are called "general denials." This means that in its answer, the defendant can simply deny allegations without elaborating. The defendant, however, must list all the "affirmative" defenses that apply or he risks losing them forever. So, if you have an ordinary course defense or any other kind of defense, your lawyer should assert it in the answer.

5.3 The First Hearing

The court schedules the first pretrial/status conference.[289]

At this meeting, there is usually no substantive discussion of the trustee's allegations or the defendant's defenses. Typically, the plaintiff, reading from a list, says who filed answers and who didn't. The judge may set some deadlines for the case or direct the plaintiff to submit a proposed order for deadlines. That's pretty much it. It's basically a procedural hearing.

5.4 The 26(f) Conference

There is a rule found in the Federal Rules of Civil Procedure as well as in the Federal Rules of Bankruptcy Procedure that requires a telephone conference early in the case between the plaintiff's lawyer and the defendant's lawyer.[290] The purpose of the call is to discuss the discovery needs of both sides so that the parties can come up with a reasonable plan for discovery.

Congress set up a system for federal litigation based on a simple concept. The concept is to require opposing sides to exchange information. The theory is that the exchange of information will flesh out and narrow the

---

288. *See* Fed. R. Bankr. P. 7012 ("Defenses and Objections").

289. *See* 11 U.S.C. § 105(d); *see also* Novica Petrovski, LL.M. thesis: *The Bankruptcy Code, Section 1121: Exclusivity Reloaded*, 11 Am. Bankr. Inst. L. Rev. 451, 517 (2003) ("Section 105(d) of the Bankruptcy Code grants a bankruptcy judge authority to hold a status conference and issue an order at any such conference prescribing limitations and conditions that the court deems appropriate to ensure that a case is handled expeditiously and economically.").

290. *See* Fed. R. Civ. P. 26(f) ("Conference of the Parties; Planning for Discovery"); *see also* Fed. R. Bankr. P. 7026 ("General Provisions Regarding Discovery").

issues and result in settlement of most cases. The system works well, and cases rarely go to trial.[291] In summary, we want both the plaintiff and the defendant to flip up their cards and make reasonable decisions.[292]

In preference clawback litigation, both sides, if they are seasoned at all, know exactly the kind of evidence they need. Typically, for example, the plaintiff will want to see emails to unearth collection pressure. The defendant will often voluntarily produce evidence of the history of transactions between the parties. There are seldom any surprises.

For that reason, some courts specifically waive the requirement for this initial discovery call as a waste of time.[293] Sometimes it *is* a waste of time. On the other hand, it is a pretext to start discussing possible settlement and to informally flesh out the issues and see if any immediate progress can be made.[294] In my practice, sometimes a brief discussion has resulted in the dismissal of the case after specific requested information or documentation is quickly produced.

5.5   The Parties Agree on Some Deadlines, and the Court Sets Some Deadlines[295]

In a routine preference matter, the lawyers usually agree on some deadlines, and the court often signs off on them. In a routine case, the court typically approves two or three months for exchanging evidence and other discovery. The judge might also insist on scheduling mandatory mediation.[296] After mediation, either party can usually move for "sum-

---

291. Manuel D. Leal, *Discovery Under Bankruptcy Procedure: A "Trap Door?,"* 84 N.D. L. Rev. 111, 119 (2008) (stating that as a result of the discovery process, "attorneys may be apprised of the strength and weaknesses not only of their opponent's side but also of their own. The liberality of the discovery rules permits litigants to seriously consider settlement, and at the very least, expedite the administration of justice.").

292. *Id.*

293. *See* Mendelsohn v. Gordon (*In re* Who's Who Worldwide Registry, Inc.), 197 B.R. 193 (Bankr. E.D.N.Y. 1996) (featuring trustee who agreed to waive discovery in his adversary proceeding and court enjoining discovery).

294. Leal, *supra* note 293, at 119 (stating that as a result of the discovery process, "attorneys may be apprised of the strength and weaknesses not only of their opponent's side but also of their own. The liberality of the discovery rules permits litigants to seriously consider settlement, and at the very least, expedite the administration of justice.").

295. *See* Fed. R. Civ. P. 16(b) ("Scheduling"); *see also* Fed. R. Bankr. P. 7016 ("Pre-Trial Procedure").

296. William J. Woodward, Jr., *ADR Meets Bankruptcy: Cross-Purposes or Cross-Pollination?: The Third Way: Mediation of Products Claims in the Piper Aircraft Trust,* 17 Am. Bankr. Inst. L. Rev. 463 (2009) ("In 2007, Bankruptcy Judge Stephen Rhoads ordered some 1,170 bankruptcy preference actions brought by a debtor into a mandatory mediation

mary judgment."[297] If none of that works to resolve the case, then a trial date is set.[298]

5.6 Discovery

In most civil litigation in federal court, the parties will serve written discovery demands on each other.[299]

5.6.1 Document Demands

In the case of clawback litigation, the defendant might want to see any emails or letters that seem to apply unusual collection pressure. As we saw above, extraordinary collection pressure might destroy an ordinary course defense, which makes it likely that the plaintiff will want this kind of documentation from the defendant. The defendant also wants it, to avoid being sandbagged by the plaintiff springing this destructive evidence in a motion or at trial.

Once a plaintiff sent me a document entitled "Preferred Vendors" that was a list of vendors the debtor had decided to single out for payment while not paying other vendors. My client was on the list. Not good, but like Don Corleone in *The Godfather*, I insist on hearing bad news right away.

5.6.2 Interrogatories

These are a bunch of written questions both sides ask each other that must be answered in writing.[300] For example, a defendant might want to know if the debtor owns the real estate on which the defendant is asserting a hypothetical lien.

---

program . . . . Earlier, in 2004, the District Court of Delaware instituted a mandatory mediation program. . . ."); for an example of a successful mandatory mediation program, see *In re* Piper Aircraft Corp., 162 B.R. 619 (Bankr. S.D. Fla. 1994).

297. *See* Fed. R. Civ. P. 56 ("Summary Judgment"); *see also* Fed. R. Bankr. P. 7056 ("Summary Judgment").

298. *See* Fed. R. Civ. P. 16(b)(3)(B)(iv).

299. *See* Fed. R. Civ. P. 34; *see also* Fed. R. Bankr. P. 7034.

300. *See* Fed R. Civ. P. 33; *see also* Fed. R. Bankr. P. 7033.

5.6.3 Request for Admissions

This is a document consisting of a list of statements that a party is requesting the other side to either admit or deny.[301] The rule is that if they are not denied, they are automatically admitted.[302] In the context of preference litigation, these are, most of the time, pretty silly. For example, I will ask the plaintiff to admit that all payments were made in the ordinary course. Unless I catch the plaintiff's lawyer smoking crack, he is going to deny this statement.

Both sides, I think, send these out on the off chance that the other side will make a mistake. For example, if I don't respond within 30 days, everything the plaintiff wants to be admitted will be deemed admitted. If that happens, the plaintiff has gained some settlement leverage. However, most courts will allow you to make a motion to withdraw your admissions.[303] Occasionally, though, you could get a judge in a bad mood and lose your entire case by missing one deadline. I take requests for admissions very seriously for that reason. It's one of the very few "gotcha!" traps in bankruptcy litigation.

5.7   Mediation

A mediator is usually a lawyer who applied to be on a list of available mediators and was court-approved as a mediator.[304] The mediator is often a bankruptcy lawyer burnt out by constant conflict and deadlines who is seeking a less stressful way to earn a living.[305] Mediation in bankruptcy court is nonbinding.[306] This means that all you need do is show up and

---

301. *See* Fed. R. Civ. P. 36; *see also* Fed. R. Bankr. P. 7036.

302. *See* Fed. R. Civ. P. 36(a)(4).

303. *See* Fed. R. Civ. P. 36(b).

304. William J. Woodward, Jr., *Evaluating Bankruptcy Mediation*, 1999 J. Disp. Resol. 1, 6 (1999) ("In simplest terms, mediation is the use of a third party to assist parties to a dispute in reaching compromise. In its purest form, the mediator simply aids the parties in clarifying the issues and the parties' respective positions.").

305. Lisa A. Lomax, *Alternative Dispute Resolution in Bankruptcy: Rule 9019 and Bankruptcy Mediation Programs*, 68 Am. Bankr. L.J. 55, 72 (1994) (opining that "legal training and substantial experience in bankruptcy are necessary attributes of a successful mediator").

306. Ralph R. Mabey, Charles J. Tabb, & Ira S. Dizengoff, *Expanding the Reach of Alternative Dispute Resolution in Bankruptcy: The Legal and Practical Bases for the Use of Mediation and the Other Forms of ADR*, 46 S.C. L. Rev. 1259, 1288-89 (1995) ("Section 105 of the Bankruptcy Code provides important statutory authority for the use of nonbinding

negotiate "in good faith"—whatever that means.

In practice, you meet with the trustee, the trustee's lawyer, your lawyer, and the mediator in a conference room. The plaintiff's lawyer gives his opening statement and does some "posturing." Posturing involves making false statements as a negotiating position. Here are some examples:

- We will never, in a million years, go below $X.

- If we don't get a settlement today, we are going to push toward trial immediately.

- We will push toward trial, and a trial will cost you $X amount in legal fees.

- We have not settled any cases for less than $X, and we are not about to start now.

- You have zero chance of winning on your ordinary course defense.

- You are very unreasonable by not settling for $X.

- You are acting in "bad faith" by not settling for $X.

- We are going to move for summary judgment tomorrow if this case doesn't settle for $X.

After the plaintiff's lawyer is finished, I mirror his statement with my own. After this time-wasting ritual, the plaintiff's lawyer, his client, and the mediator will go into another office.

The mediator will then begin shuttle diplomacy. He will speak with the trustee and try to get a settlement number. He will talk to us to try to get a settlement number. Then he will go back and forth and attempt to bridge the gap.

Trustees and plaintiffs' counsel sue a lot of folks. Because they sue a lot of folks, they give a lot of business to mediators. This is especially true in places like Delaware where mediation is required in most cases. Me-

---

[mediation] procedures in bankruptcy cases[;] . . . section 105(d) of the Bankruptcy Code, added by the Bankruptcy Reform Act of 1994, provides statutory support for the use of mandatory nonbinding [mediation] procedures in bankruptcy cases . . . .").

diators, being human, tend to have warm feelings for people on whom their livelihood depends. Of course, mediators strive to be neutral and professional, but they are not robots.[307]

In my experience, the mediator will tend to pressure the defendant to settle the case on terms more favorable to the plaintiff than to the defendant. Preference defendants do not trust the plaintiff's lawyer. They typically have some trust for their own lawyer but not that much. They want to trust the mediator.

In my opinion, though, mediators work for the plaintiff. They often convince the defendant to enter into some terrible deals despite my protests. In Delaware, the trustee/plaintiff is required to pay the entire bill of the mediator. You work for the person who pays you.

5.8   Settlement

Once your lawyers agree on a number at mediation or later on the phone or by email, the agreement needs to be reduced to writing and sometimes approved by the court.[308]

The steps are as follows:

- The lawyers agree on the dollar amount that will settle the case.

- The lawyers agree or disagree about whether you are going to give up your claim against the estate.

- A "Settlement Stipulation" is drafted, approved, and executed by all parties, including you.[309]

---

307. Lomax, *supra* note 307, at 77-78 (discussing potential conflicts of interest of bankruptcy mediators).

308. *Id.* at 87-88 ("Settlements reached through mediation must be approved by the court under rule 9019(a) if they affect the estate. . . . [N]otice must be given to the other creditors so that they can review the settlement and make any objections prior to its approval by the court."); *see also* Fed. R. Bankr. P. 9019(a).

309. Mabey, Tabb, & Dizengoff, *supra* note 308, at 1282 ("If the parties do reach settlement, the parties must submit the executed stipulation agreement to the court for approval, usually within a short period of time.").

- The plaintiff files a motion with the court asking that the Stipulation be approved.[310]

- The court usually approves the Stipulation and closes the case.

5.8.1.1 Settling Your Case

Resolving preference cases is 50% negotiation and 50% legal analysis. A lot of the negotiation involves both sides exaggerating the strengths of their case and minimizing its weaknesses. It is vital for the defendant's attorney to convince the plaintiff that he (the plaintiff) has a shaky case. The more the plaintiff is uncertain about prevailing, the more the plaintiff will discount from the face amount of the complaint.

Many plaintiffs' attorneys use a simple formula. If the case is 80% likely to be won, then the plaintiff will settle for 80% of the face amount of the complaint. If the plaintiff has a 20% chance of winning, then the plaintiff will sell for 20% of the face amount of the complaint.

For that reason, I routinely spend a lot more time and effort arguing the case to the plaintiff than I do submitting the case to a judge. By first focusing on convincing the plaintiff to dismiss the case or settle it for a reasonable amount, I can save the following motion practice costs:

- the cost of drafting formal briefs to be submitted to the court

- the cost of providing formal lists of exhibits

- the cost of providing copies to multiple parties including the judge

- the cost of responding to the plaintiff's formal objection if we file a formal motion in court

- the cost of preparing for oral argument in court

- the cost of attending a hearing in court, including travel time

310. *Id.*; *see also* Reynolds v. Commissioner of Internal Revenue, 861 F.2d 469, 473 (6th Cir. 1988) ("In bankruptcy proceedings, as distinguished from ordinary civil cases, any compromise between the debtor and his creditors must be approved by the court as fair and equitable. . . . The need for this safeguard is obvious. Any settlement between the debtor and one of his individual creditors necessarily affects the rights of other creditors by reducing the assets of the estate available to satisfy other creditors' claims.").

- the ever-present uncertainty when we present a case in court

Besides the fear of losing a case in court and disappointing a client, the plaintiff also has other concerns. These concerns are all-important in our attempt to create leverage for the best possible settlement. Plaintiff's concerns are as follows:

- Is prosecuting this case worth the amount of hourly billing it's going to take? It doesn't make a lot of sense to spend $15,000 to win a $20,000 preference case.

- If I win the case, does the defendant have the assets to pay a judgment?

- Is there enough money in the bankruptcy estate to pay me to litigate this case?

- If I'm handling this case on contingency, how much time is it worth?

5.8.1.2 Negotiation Tips

Preparation and timing are crucial in obtaining maximum negotiating leverage and the best possible outcome in a settlement negotiation.

If you want to woo your wife, you don't interrupt her when she's brushing her teeth or late for work. You approach her after presenting flowers, dimming the lights, and putting on some Sinatra. The same importance of preparation and timing is true when contacting plaintiff counsel to obtain the best possible settlement.

What follows are my tips for putting the trustee's lawyer in a cooperative mood:

- Prepare. Prepare. Prepare.

- You catch more bees with honey than with vinegar.

- Have both a carrot and a stick.

- The last moment is when decisions are made.

- Use the no-money defense.

5.8.1.2.1 Preparation

Plaintiffs' lawyers ignore unsupported statements like "this is not a preference" or "these payments were in the ordinary course." They are interested in one thing—bringing as much money as possible back into the bankruptcy estate. On the other hand, they don't want to waste their time. If you can convince them that you have strong defenses, you might get their attention.

If the case is solid for the defendant, you are doing the plaintiff a favor by doing your homework and presenting the evidence to him in a professional manner.

Without a professional analysis based on case precedent and the appropriate documentation, plaintiff's counsel will give you the cold shoulder.

5.8.1.2.2 Catch More Bees with Honey

You don't wrestle with a pig because you just get dirty and the pig loves it.

Making things difficult for the other lawyer merely increases his billable hours. Also, he will respond by making things more difficult for you, which will end up costing you money.

I always hope the plaintiff will focus on pursuing lower-hanging fruit. I define lower-lying fruit as other defendants he is suing that have unprepared or inexperienced counsel. These folks, and there are many out there, usually pay two to three times what is necessary to settle preference cases. Let the trustee and his counsel get high payments from 90% of his other cases.

When I approach the trustee's counsel for settlement talks, I want him to feel fat and happy.

5.8.1.2.3 Dents in the Case

Negotiating a preference settlement is like buying a used car. You complain to the dealer that the tires are shot, and there are dents on the hood. The dealer agrees to a discount. In a preference case, if you can show the dents in the plaintiff's case, you will get a discount.

5.8.1.2.4 Timing

Plaintiffs tend to give better deals the longer you wait. I'm not sure why. It might be that they settled most of their other cases and they're being encouraged by the judge to resolve the ones that remain open. Maybe dealing with you has just gotten tedious and frustrating.

5.8.1.2.5 The No-Money Defense

"I already spent that money" is not a defense. I carefully searched the Bankruptcy Code, and the I-spent-the-money defense was nowhere to be found.

"I have no money," however, is a defense of sorts. The plaintiff's lawyer's reaction to the no-money defense is usually twofold:

- First, the plaintiff will demand broad and sworn financial statements including the last three years of bank statements and tax returns. They will then rummage through your confidential information and argue on the slightest pretext that you'll be getting money shortly or that perhaps you're hiding money.

- Second, even if it's clear that you have no money, plaintiffs' lawyers often demand a default judgment (you agree to lose the case officially). They will reason that if you have no money, you won't put up a fight because you won't care about getting a judgment entered against you, and they may as well get a judgment in case you have money someday.

The best strategy is to show that you have no money and, even if you did, the plaintiff would probably lose the case. This one-two punch strategy may work well. So, it's worth submitting financial statements *if you have a strong case.* Plaintiffs' sometimes do dismiss cases without demanding a default judgment if you have no money *and* defenses.

CHAPTER 6

Why These Laws Don't Work and a Proposal for Change

6.1   The Side Effects of the Preference Law "Cure"

I have explained the rationales for the preference laws and what defenses you have against them. I have also pointed out ways that the laws are unfair:

- They are applied retroactively with no notice.

- They discourage workout arrangements.

- They may result in *less* money being paid to unsecured creditors.

In this chapter, I'll point out some other, less obvious, problems with the preference laws and how I think they should be changed.

6.2   Six More Reasons to Not Like the Preference Laws

What else is wrong with the preference laws? What follows are the list of my grievances.

6.2.1   The Preference Laws Promote Dishonesty

When a corporate debtor files for bankruptcy, it must list all creditors that it paid within the 90-day period before the filing.[311] So its bankruptcy lawyers probably know they will at some point sue vendors for clawbacks.

The last thing management wants to do is alienate vendors when the company is trying to recover. Management typically conceals, or at least does not reveal, the intention to file these potential lawsuits until the very last moment.

Vendors will probably get a plan of reorganization and a disclosure statement that they will vote on to approve the reorganization.[312] The debtor not only wants vendors to continue supplying goods and services. It also wants vendors to vote for its plan.

Clawback lawsuits are quietly held back. Often, they are intentionally filed at the very last moment—usually the day before the expiration of the two-year statute of limitations. Vendors find out later that they were sandbagged—they voted unknowingly for the very plan that, in small print, made provisions for a trustee to sue them.

The mealy-mouthed defense is that a provision for future clawback lawsuits is disclosed in the Disclosure Statement and Plan of Reorganization. True. But these documents are typically hundreds of pages of indecipherable legal small print mumbo-jumbo. This is not real or appropriate disclosure.

This calculating subterfuge is dismaying since bankruptcy proceedings are meant to be, and for the most part are, transparent proceedings.[313]

6.2.2   The Preference Laws Are Procedurally Unfair

The Bankruptcy Code and Federal Rules of Bankruptcy Procedure permit the plaintiff in preference clawback cases to sue defendants

---

311. *See* 11 U.S.C. § 521 (setting forth the debtor's duties, including filing a list of creditors).

312. *See* Union Carbide Corp. v. Newboles, 686 F.2d 593, 595 (7th Cir. 1982) ("[A] majority of the creditors must approve the debtor's plan for the debtor to be discharged . . . .").

313. Lipson, *supra* note 43, at 1618 (2009) ("Transparency has long been a vital feature of reorganization under Chapter 11 . . . . 'The key' to successful reorganization under Chapter 11, the Second Circuit famously observed in the Lionel case, 'is disclosure.'" (citing Committee of Equity Security Holders v. Lionel Corp. (*In re* Lionel Corp.), 722 F.2d 1063, 1070 (2d Cir. 1983))).

no matter where they are located. While many companies form their corporations in New York or Delaware, they may do business in North Dakota or Georgia or some other distant state.

Vendors located throughout the country are forced to hire lawyers in New York or Delaware or elsewhere. They may need to attend court hearings or mediation thousands of miles from their homes and businesses. They must stay in hotels, pay for airplane tickets, and miss work time. [314] The unwelcome news is that you can be sued in a faraway venue is also without notice since people assume that if there were any litigation, it would be held where the business was conducted.

Instead, preference case plaintiffs in New York or Delaware routinely shock a lot of folks by hauling them into court from all over the place, even from other countries.

The plaintiff, on the other hand, suffers no inconvenience since she can often walk to the courthouse from her office.

Lastly, there is an even more critical home court advantage. The trustee and plaintiff's counsel has typically had a lot of face time with an essential person—the judge presiding over the case. They have often earned the court's trust and respect over many years. Lawyers for defendants, on the other hand, are often strangers who just rode into town. Judges are usually fair and impartial. But it looks one-sided and sketchy, especially to a non-lawyer.

6.2.3   The Preference Laws' Triple Whammy

Trustees bring preference cases after businesses go bankrupt. Companies often go bankrupt in either a general recession or an industry-specific slump.[315]

So, you're more likely to get sued in a preference case when your business is bad for both you and the debtor.

---

314. A number of defendants have filed "objection to venue" motions, but the way the law has developed, these are pretty much always denied.

315. *Collier on Bankruptcy* App. Pt. 4(c) at 48 (16th ed. 2017) ("There is ample evidence demonstrating that economic recessions do have a substantial impact on the number of bankruptcy cases, both business and nonbusiness.").

Vendors get hit with a triple whammy:

- The first whammy is that the debtor probably didn't pay you in full, and you probably really needed the money since your whole industry may be suffering.[316]

- The second whammy is that you get sued for a preference clawback. Not only did the debtor not pay you in full, but now you must return somehow whatever money you were paid, which you probably already spent.

- The third whammy is that a good customer went bankrupt and you lost that revenue stream.

The result of the triple whammy is that businesses that can't pay preference liabilities will themselves go bankrupt. These newly bankrupt companies will, in turn, sue other companies for preferences and so on. It's like a bad zombie movie.

Far from benefiting unsecured creditors, the preference laws create a vicious cycle of collapsing small businesses at a time of economic vulnerability.

6.2.4 The Preference Laws Encourage Bad Business Decisions

Preferential treatment of vendors is not always bad. In fact, it may save a business. If you own a steakhouse in financial trouble, you will prioritize paying the butcher. When cash is limited, you must favor vendors that will keep you in business. That way, you can save employees and eventually pay all vendors in full.

But Congress, in its wisdom, had other ideas about how to run a business. Most of the preferential payments that I've seen were made for excellent reasons. Reversing these payments is reversing rational decision-making. By discouraging troubled firms from favoring essential vendors, Congress is creating more bankruptcies, not fewer.

---

316. *Id.*

6.2.5   The Preference Laws Appear Arbitrary and Often Absurd

A vendor that got paid 91 days before the bankruptcy petition is exempt from the preference laws while others paid within the 90-day period are punished. While I understand that Congress must draw a line somewhere, this line seems particularly arbitrary. Perhaps there should be no 90-day window at all, and some other criteria should replace it. Maybe there should be a requirement of clear intent by the debtor to file for bankruptcy before any preference period commences.

Also, often all or almost all vendors get sued for preferences. If all or most vendors get paid in the 90-day period, how could any *one* of them be preferred? *All* unsecured creditors are being sued to protect . . . *all* unsecured creditors!

When all or most unsecured creditors are sued, the fig leaf rationale that we are helping unsecured creditors drops away. This is especially true if the clawback cash that should go to unsecured creditors is secretly siphoned off to pay bankruptcy lawyer invoices, big bank debts or who knows what.

This inherent absurdity might be resolved by prohibiting preference lawsuits when the clear majority of unsecured creditors got paid within the 90-day period.

6.2.6   The Preference Laws Themselves Create Preferential Treatment

The raison d'être of the preference laws is to prevent some vendors being preferred over other vendors. But the preference laws fight preferential treatment by substituting another form of preferential treatment. The laws favor some creditors and deem them exempt from clawback lawsuits:[317]

- If you get paid soon after shipping your product the contemporaneous exchange defense exempts you.

---

317. Mark J. Roe & Frederick Tung, *Breaking Bankruptcy Priority: How Rent-Seeking Upends the Creditors' Bargain*, 99 Va. L. Rev. 1235, 1244 (2013) ("Bankruptcy-specific rules prioritize favored creditors, such as tax authorities and employees claiming unpaid back wages, as well as offering priority to the post-bankruptcy suppliers of credit, goods, and

- If you are a fully secured creditor, you cannot be sued for a preference.

- If you are a utility and paid like clockwork, you likely have an iron-clad defense.

If we draft laws that prevent debtors from preferring particular creditors, it is hypocritical that those same laws arbitrarily prefer certain *other* creditors.

6.3   A Radical Proposal for Change

6.3.1   The Real Problem Is Not Inequality of Treatment

The current laws "fix" a problem, inequality of treatment, that very few creditors care about. What creditors might care about is a situation where someone is intentionally and with bad faith getting an unfair advantage.

Preferential prebankruptcy payments can be sorted into five categories:

- *Nobody knows anything.* The debtor's management has no idea that it will be filing a bankruptcy petition in three months and has no intention whatsoever of preferring any particular creditor. The preferred creditor knows nothing about a looming bankruptcy. This is probably the most common situation.

- *Only the debtor knows, and his heart is in the right place.* The debtor knows he might put his company for bankruptcy in three months and decides to pay a particular creditor because that creditor provides a product or service that can keep him in business and maybe turn things around. The creditor knows nothing. This is the second most common situation.

---

services necessary to rehabilitate the debtor. As bankruptcy distribution moves down the priority ladder, it eventually reaches the first unfortunate class that does not receive full payment; creditors in this class share proportionately in the value remaining, and lower priority classes receive nothing.").

- *The debtor knows and plays favorites for no good reason.* The debtor's owner knows she will be filing for bankruptcy and decides to pay a creditor because she is a close friend of that creditor. The creditor knows nothing. I have never seen this happen. If the debtor decides to prefer a creditor, it's almost always for a business reason.

- *The debtor knows, and the creditor also knows, but there is no conspiracy.* For example, the debtor's owner knows he will put the company for bankruptcy within three months, and the creditor is somehow tipped off. Not being a fool, the creditor increases his collection pressure and gets paid before the bankruptcy. My guess is that this happens about 10% of the time.

- *There is a conspiracy between the debtor and the creditor for no good reason.* The debtor knows she's about to file for bankruptcy and calls the creditor and tells that creditor about the imminent bankruptcy. Both expressly agree that the creditor will get paid in full before the bankruptcy. I would say this happens less than 1% of the time. I have never seen this situation occur.

In the first three categories, the creditor is innocent of trying to get paid ahead of his fellow creditors. After defending clawback cases for twenty years, I am confident most vendors would agree with me that it's better to permit some innocent preferred vendors to keep the money rather than permit a trustee to sue all vendors in every bankruptcy case.

It's unfair that some creditors get full payment while other creditors may end up getting paid very little.[318] But it's not *fairer* to force innocent creditors to return those funds. (Especially, where unsecured creditors may end up with no benefit anyway from those clawbacks.) Lawmakers' attempts to fix this unfixable mess have just made matters worse.

---

318. Weisberg, *supra* note 52, at 119-20 ("'The cornerstone of the [Bankruptcy Code's] preference section is the principle of equality of distribution based on fairness and perhaps economic utility.' . . . [S]ection 547 comes closer to the principle that 'all creditors ought to be treated equally.'" (quoting Ward & Shulman, *In Defense of the Bankruptcy Code's Radical Integration of the Preference Rules Affecting Commercial Financing*, 61 Wash. U. L.Q. 1, 16-18 (1983))).

The last two categories are different. The creditor is not innocent. That creditor is *intentionally* gaining an advantage over other creditors. If a creditor knows there will be a bankruptcy and acts with that knowledge to get an advantage, then the fairness needle tilts away from him. It seems fair to force a return of the payment.

Inequality of distribution might be unfair, but when accidental it's not *that* unfair. It falls under the category of "stuff happens." What's very unfair, though, is when some scheming creditors use superior knowledge to get a secret, unfair advantage. I base this on my gut feeling about justice.

The above being the case, I suggest that the preference laws need a brand new paradigm.

6.3.2 Insider Trading Laws Do a Better Job of Remedying Unfairness

Insider trading laws are designed to prevent people from exploiting an unfair advantage. In the context of securities law, that unfair advantage is secret nonpublic knowledge.[319]

In the bankruptcy world, creditors that have nonpublic knowledge of an impending bankruptcy and use that information to get paid before the bankruptcy also have an unfair advantage.

The elements of a prosecution of unlawful insider trading are

- trading

- while in possession of

- material

- nonpublic information.[320]

---

319. Stephen Clark, *Insider Trading and Financial Economics: Where Do We Go from Here?* 16 Stan. J.L. Bus. & Fin. 43, 47 (2010) ("Illegal insider trading refers to the buying or selling of a security by an insider or a 'tippee,' in violation of a fiduciary or other relationship of trust and confidence, while in possession of material, nonpublic information about the security. The purpose of prohibiting such trading is to ensure that markets are fair by precluding trading by those who have special knowledge that is not available to other traders.").

320. *See* 15 U.S.C. § 78; *see also* 17 C.F.R. § 240.10b-5.

The law does not require proof of bad intent.

The insider trading laws don't allow the SEC to sue everyone who bought stock within 90 days before a stock shot up. They focus on the most critical issue: the use of nonpublic insider information to get an unfair advantage.[321]

A creditor who uses nonpublic information about an upcoming bankruptcy to get paid ahead of other creditors is *precisely* like an investor who uses nonpublic information to buy stocks. Both gain an unfair advantage based on secret information. The difference is that the securities laws punish bad actors. The preference laws often punish innocent unsecured creditors.[322]

6.3.3   My Proposal

I propose that the preference laws be repealed, and new rules be enacted. These laws would make it a misdemeanor to receive payment by a debtor while the creditor was in possession of material nonpublic information about the debtor's imminent bankruptcy.[323] My proposed laws would also require the return of the preference plus sanctions in an amount triple the size of the preferential payment.

Replacing the preference laws with a statute similar to the insider trading laws would have the following benefits:

- The laws would only target those preferential creditors with special nonpublic knowledge.

- The laws would leave untouched debtor transfers that help the debtor's business, such as workout agreements or debtor decisions to pay critical vendors.

- The laws would allow transfers to creditors that were indeed in the ordinary course in the ordinary sense of that phrase.

---

321. Clark, *supra* note 321, at 47 ("Insider trading is legal once the material information has been made public, at which time the insider has no direct advantage over other investors.").

322. In most cases the "defenses" are so expensive to assert that as a practical matter almost all defendants incur some financial pain regardless of the strength of the defenses even if only to the lawyer defending the matter.

323. That is, the creditors described in the fourth and fifth categories in Section 6.3.1.

- The laws would apply to all creditors and eliminate preferential treatment of secured or other creditors.

- While the law would still be applied retroactively, it would be implemented against folks who know they are in the wrong and who would not be surprised at being brought to justice.

- The laws would be an effective deterrent.[324]

I urge any legislators who are reading to consider the above.

---

324. Since the money recouped often does not benefit unsecured creditors anyway, deterrence should be the primary goal.

CHAPTER 7

Appendix[324]

7.1   Appendix A. Section 547 of the Bankruptcy Code

§547. Preferences

(a) In this section—

(1) "inventory" means personal property leased or furnished, held for sale or lease, or to be furnished under a contract for service, raw materials, work in process, or materials used or consumed in a business, including farm products such as crops or livestock, held for sale or lease;

(2) "new value" means money or money's worth in goods, services, or new credit, or release by a transferee of property previously transferred to such transferee in a transaction that is neither void nor voidable by the debtor or the trustee under any applicable law, including proceeds of such property, but does not include an obligation substituted for an existing obligation;

(3) "receivable" means right to payment, whether or not such right has been earned by performance; and

(4) a debt for a tax is incurred on the day when such tax is last payable

---

325. Disclaimer: Any names, characters, places, and incidents mentioned in the Appendixes below either are products of the author's imagination or are used fictitiously. Any resemblance to actual events or locales or persons, living or dead, is entirely coincidental. The document is created only to be used for basic understanding of various pleadings and to give an idea of a format which is generally being used in various preference lawsuits.

without penalty, including any extension.

(b) Except as provided in subsections (c) and (i) of this section, the trustee may avoid any transfer of an interest of the debtor in property—

(1) to or for the benefit of a creditor;

(2) for or on account of an antecedent debt owed by the debtor before such transfer was made;

(3) made while the debtor was insolvent;

(4) made—

(A) on or within 90 days before the date of the filing of the petition; or

(B) between ninety days and one year before the date of the filing of the petition, if such creditor at the time of such transfer was an insider; and

(5) that enables such creditor to receive more than such creditor would receive if—

(A) the case were a case under chapter 7 of this title;

(B) the transfer had not been made; and

(C) such creditor received payment of such debt to the extent provided by the provisions of this title.

(c) The trustee may not avoid under this section a transfer—

(1) to the extent that such transfer was—

(A) intended by the debtor and the creditor to or for whose benefit such transfer was made to be a contemporaneous exchange for new value given to the debtor; and

(B) in fact a substantially contemporaneous exchange;

(2) to the extent that such transfer was in payment of a debt incurred by the debtor in the ordinary course of business or financial affairs of the debtor and the transferee, and such transfer was—

Appendix

(A) made in the ordinary course of business or financial affairs of the debtor and the transferee; or

(B) made according to ordinary business terms;

(3) that creates a security interest in property acquired by the debtor—

(A) to the extent such security interest secures new value that was—

(i) given at or after the signing of a security agreement that contains a description of such property as collateral;

(ii) given by or on behalf of the secured party under such agreement;

(iii) given to enable the debtor to acquire such property; and

(iv) in fact used by the debtor to acquire such property; and

(B) that is perfected on or before 30 days after the debtor receives possession of such property;

(4) to or for the benefit of a creditor, to the extent that, after such transfer, such creditor gave new value to or for the benefit of the debtor—

(A) not secured by an otherwise unavoidable security interest; and

(B) on account of which new value the debtor did not make an otherwise unavoidable transfer to or for the benefit of such creditor;

(5) that creates a perfected security interest in inventory or a receivable or the proceeds of either, except to the extent that the aggregate of all such transfers to the transferee caused a reduction, as of the date of the filing of the petition and to the prejudice of other creditors holding unsecured claims, of any amount by which the debt secured by such security interest exceeded the value of all security interests for such debt on the later of—

(A)(i) with respect to a transfer to which subsection (b)(4)(A) of this section applies, 90 days before the date of the filing of the petition; or

(ii) with respect to a transfer to which subsection (b)(4)(B) of this section applies, one year before the date of the filing of the petition; or

(B) the date on which new value was first given under the security agreement creating such security interest;

(6) that is the fixing of a statutory lien that is not avoidable under section 545 of this title;

(7) to the extent such transfer was a bona fide payment of a debt for a domestic support obligation;

(8) if, in a case filed by an individual debtor whose debts are primarily consumer debts, the aggregate value of all property that constitutes or is affected by such transfer is less than $600; or

(9) if, in a case filed by a debtor whose debts are not primarily consumer debts, the aggregate value of all property that constitutes or is affected by such transfer is less than $5,000.

(d) The trustee may avoid a transfer of an interest in property of the debtor transferred to or for the benefit of a surety to secure reimbursement of such a surety that furnished a bond or other obligation to dissolve a judicial lien that would have been avoidable by the trustee under subsection (b) of this section. The liability of such surety under such bond or obligation shall be discharged to the extent of the value of such property recovered by the trustee or the amount paid to the trustee.

(e)(1) For the purposes of this section—

(A) a transfer of real property other than fixtures, but including the interest of a seller or purchaser under a contract for the sale of real property, is perfected when a bona fide purchaser of such property from the debtor against whom applicable law permits such transfer to be perfected cannot acquire an interest that is superior to the interest of the transferee; and

(B) a transfer of a fixture or property other than real property is perfected when a creditor on a simple contract cannot acquire a judicial lien that is superior to the interest of the transferee.

(2) For the purposes of this section, except as provided in paragraph (3) of this subsection, a transfer is made—

(A) at the time such transfer takes effect between the transferor and the transferee, if such transfer is perfected at, or within 30 days after, such time, except as provided in subsection (c)(3)(B);

(B) at the time such transfer is perfected, if such transfer is perfected after such 30 days; or

(C) immediately before the date of the filing of the petition, if such transfer is not perfected at the later of—

(i) the commencement of the case; or

(ii) 30 days after such transfer takes effect between the transferor and the transferee.

(3) For the purposes of this section, a transfer is not made until the debtor has acquired rights in the property transferred.

(f) For the purposes of this section, the debtor is presumed to have been insolvent on and during the 90 days immediately preceding the date of the filing of the petition.

(g) For the purposes of this section, the trustee has the burden of proving the avoidability of a transfer under subsection (b) of this section, and the creditor or party in interest against whom recovery or avoidance is sought has the burden of proving the nonavoidability of a transfer under subsection (c) of this section.

(h) The trustee may not avoid a transfer if such transfer was made as a part of an alternative repayment schedule between the debtor and any creditor of the debtor created by an approved nonprofit budget and credit counseling agency.

(i) If the trustee avoids under subsection (b) a transfer made between 90 days and 1 year before the date of the filing of the petition, by the debtor to an entity that is not an insider for the benefit of a creditor that is an insider, such transfer shall be considered to be avoided under this section only with respect to the creditor that is an insider.

7.2 Appendix B. Sample Demand Letter for Preference Payment Recovery

Laurel, Harry and Moser, LLP
999 Livestreet Road
Wilmington, Delaware

April 1, 2013

Jim Jack
Suite No. 1000
42nd Milestone St.
New York. NY

RE: Preference Demand In re: Acme E. terpi. ~, Inc., Case No. 11-0000 (MUW)

Dear Creditor:

The undersigned represents Jim Jone. 'the "Trustee"), not individually but solely as the Chapter 7 trustee of the ba .'ruptcy estate of Acme Enterprises, Inc., et al. (the "Debtor").

As you may already know, or November 12, 2012 (the "Petition Date"), the Debtor filed a petition for relief pursuant to Chapter 11 of the Bankruptcy Code and operated its business as a Chapter 11 debtor and debtor in possession until the closing of sale of substantially all of its operating assets to a third party on November 17, 2012. The Debtor's bankruptcy case was subsequently converted to a case pursuant to Chapter 7 of the Bankruptcy Code and Jim Jones was appointed as a trustee of the Debtor's bankruptcy estate.

Pursuant to sections 547 and 550 of the Bankruptcy Code, 11 U.S.C. §§ 547 and 550, and subject to certain defenses, transfers of the Debtor's property to or for the benefit of a creditor, for or on account of an antecedent debt, while the Debtor was insolvent, during the 90-day period preceding the Petition Date and that enable that creditor to receive more than it would have in a Chapter 7 bankruptcy case, are avoidable and recoverable.

Appendix

The Debtor's records indicate that you received payments identified totaling $99,999.99 (the "Preferential Transfers") from the Debtor during the Preference Period that appear to be recoverable by the Trustee. These Preferential Transfers are liable to be returned to the Debtor's bankruptcy estate and distributed to its creditors equally pursuant to Chapter 7 of the Bankruptcy Code.

The Trustee is preparing to initiate lawsuits to recover any avoidable transfers, including the Preferential Transfers. In order to avoid any adverse legal action against you based on the Preferential Transfers, the Trustee hereby demands the return of all of the Preferential Transfers you received from the Debtor during the Preference Period within 30 days of your receipt of this letter. Checks should be made payable to Jim Jones not individually but solely as the Trustee of the bankruptcy estate of Acme Enterprises, Inc., et al. and mailed to the address provided on the letterhead.

We have sent this letter directly to you because no attorney has entered an appearance on your behalf in the Debtor's bankruptcy case. If you have any questions or believe that you have any relevant defenses to an action to recover the Preferential Transfers, please contact the undersigned at (222) 555-111 or via email at acmepreferencetransfers@laurelharrymoser.com.

Sincerely yours,

Peter Smith, Esq.

7.3   Appendix C. Sample Complaint

IN THE UNITED STATES BANKRUPTCY COURT

FOR THE DISTRICT OF DELAWARE

In re:	Chapter 7
ACME ENTERPRISES, INC. *et al.*,[326]	Case No. 11-0000 (MUW)
Debtors.	
--	(Jointly Administered)
JIM JONES, Chapter 7 Trustee of Acme Enterprises, Inc. *et al.*,	
Plaintiff,	
vs.	Adv. Proceeding No. 15-9898-MUW
XYZ Widgets, Inc.,	
Defendant.	

---

326. The Debtors and the last four digits of their respective federal taxpayer identification numbers are as follows: Acme Enterprises, Inc. (2222); Acme Pooled Services, Inc. (6699); Universal Flyers, Inc. (5555).

Appendix

COMPLAINT FOR AVOIDANCE AND RECOVERY

OF PREFERENTIAL TRANSFERS

PURSUANT TO 11 U.S.C. §§ 547 & 550

OF THE BANKRUPTCY CODE

Plaintiff Jim Jones, Chapter 7 trustee (the "Trustee" or the "Plaintiff") for the estates of the above-captioned debtors (the "Debtors"), for his Complaint for Avoidance and Recovery of' Preferential Transfers Pursuant to 11 U.S.C. §§ 547 & 550 against XYZ Widgets Inc. (the "Defendant") alleges as follows:

Nature of the Action

1. The Plaintiff brings this action against the Defendant to avoid and recover certain preferential transfers that occurred during the 90-day period prior to commencement of the Debtor's bankruptcy case.

Jurisdiction and Venue

2. The United States Bankruptcy Court for the District of Delaware (the "Bankruptcy Court") has jurisdiction over this adversary proceeding under Chapter 11 of Title 11, United States Code (the "Bankruptcy"), pursuant to 28 U.S.C. §§ 157(a) and 1334(a).

3. This proceeding is a core proceeding within the meaning of 28 U.S.C. 157(b) and the Bankruptcy Court may enter final orders for the matters contained herein. If it is determined that the Bankruptcy Court, absent consent of the parties, cannot enter final orders or judgments herein consistent with Article III of the United States Constitution, the Plaintiff hereby consents to the entry of the final orders or judgments by the Bankruptcy Court.

4. Venue in this District is proper pursuant to 28 U.S.C. §§ 1408 and 1409(a).

5. This adversary proceeding is commenced pursuant to Rule 7001(1) of the Federal Rules of Bankruptcy Procedure and sections 547 and 550 of the Bankruptcy Code.

The Parties

6. The Trustee is the duly appointed trustee for the estates of the above-captioned Debtors. Pursuant to 11 U.S.C. § 704, the Trustee has the authority to investigate the financial affairs of the Debtors and to litigate affirmative claims of the Debtors.

7. Upon information and belief, the Defendant is a corporation formed under the laws of the State of New York that maintains its principal executive office at 1000 Air Plaza, 32nd Street, New York.

8. On November 12, 2012 (the "Petition Date"), the Debtors each commenced a case by filing a voluntary petition for relief in the Bankruptcy Court under Chapter 11 of the Bankruptcy Code (collectively, the "Cases").

9. The Cases are being jointly administered for procedural purposes pursuant to Bankruptcy Rule 1015(b) under Case Number 11-10000 (MUW).

10. On December 30, 2012, the Court entered an order converting the Cases to cases under Chapter 7 of the Bankruptcy Code [Docket No. 111].

11. On January 30, 2013, Jim Jones was appointed as the Chapter 7 Trustee [Docket No. 777].

General Allegations

12. Prior to the Petition Date, the Debtors, founded in 1918, provided military cargo, passenger, and commercial charter air services through their two airlines. The Debtors' principal offices were located at 000 Worli Drive, Stemtree City, Georgia 00001.

13. 'The Debtors were one of the largest providers of private airlift services to the U.S. Military, including both passenger and cargo services, using 24 leased aircraft. There were three business lines: (1) passenger and cargo services for commercial customers; (2) charter passenger and cargo service for the military and other government agencies; and (3) full service flying for non-military charter customers.

14. In the ordinary course of their businesses, the Debtors maintained relationships with various entities through which the Debtors regularly pur-

chased, sold, received, or delivered goods and services.

15. Prior to the Petition Date, the Defendant provided the Debtor with air charter services.

16. During the course of their relationship, the parties engaged in numerous transactions, which are reflected in purchase orders, invoices, communications, and other documents (collectively, the "Agreements"). In particular, pursuant to the Agreements, Debtor Universal Flyers would pay the Defendant for air charter services.

17. As a result, during the ninety days prior to the Petition Date, the Debtors made payments to or for the benefit of the Defendant (collectively, the "Transfers"), including those identified on Exhibit A attached hereto. Exhibit A sets forth the details of each of the Transfers, including the identity of the transferor Debtor, invoice date, invoice number, payment date, mail date, check number, and payment amount. The aggregate amount of the Transfers is not less than $ 99,999.99

18. The Plaintiff acknowledges that some Transfers may be subject to defenses under 11 U.S.C. § 547(c), upon which Defendant bears the burden of proof pursuant to 11 U.S.C. § 547(g),

First Claim for Relief

(Avoidance of Preferential Transfers-11 U.S.C. ~ 547)

19. The Plaintiff repeats and re-alleges the allegations in paragraphs 1 through 18; above, as though fully set forth at length.

20. Within the ninety days prior to the Petition Date, Debtor Universal Flyers made transfers to Defendant in the total amount of $99,999.99, as more specifically described in Exhibit A.

21. 'The Transfers to the Defendant were each a transfer of property of Debtor Universal Flyer.

22. The Transfers to the Defendant were each made to or for the benefit of the Defendant.

23. The Defendant was a creditor of Debtor Universal Flyer (within the meaning of 11 U.S.C. § 110) at the time each of the Transfers was made or, alternatively, received the transfers for the benefit of a creditor or creditors of the Debtor Universal Flyer.

24. The Transfers to the Defendant were each on account of an antecedent debt owed by Debtor Universal Flyer to the Defendant before the Transfers were made.

25. The Transfers were made while Debtor Universal Flyer was insolvent. Debtor Universal Flyer is presumed to be insolvent during the 90 days preceding the Petition Date pursuant to 11 U.S,C. § 547(f).

26. Each of the Transfers enabled the Defendant to receive more than the Defendant would have received if (i) the transfers and/or payments had not been made, and (ii) the Defendant received payment on account of the debt paid by each of the Transfers to the extent provided by the Bankruptcy Code.

27. As of the date hereof, the Defendant has not returned the Transfers to the plaintiff'.

28. The Plaintiff is entitled to an order and judgment under 11 U.S.C. § 547 that the Transfers are avoided.

Second Claim for Relief

(Recovery of Property—11 U.S.C. § 550)

29. The Plaintiff repeats and re-alleges the allegations in paragraphs 1 through 28, above, as though fully set forth at length.

30. Pursuant to 11 U.S.C. § 550(a), to the extent that a transfer is avoided under 11 U.S.C. § 547, the Plaintiff may recover for the benefit of the estate the property transferred or the value of such property from (a) the initial transferee of such transfer or the entity for whose such transfer was made or (b) any immediate or mediate transferee of such initial transferee.

31. The Defendant is either the (a) initial transferee of the Transfers, the entity for whose benefit the Transfers were made or (b) an immediate or mediate transferee of the initial transferee.

Appendix

32. Subject to the Defendant's potential defenses, the Plaintiff is entitled to recover the value of the Transfers pursuant to 11 U.S.C. § 550(a),

WHEREFORE, the Plaintiff prays for judgment as follows:

A) For a determination that the Transfers in the total amount of $99,999.99 are avoidable as preferential transfers under Section 547 of the Bankruptcy Code, and that the Plaintiff is entitled to recover the Transfers in the total amount of $99,999.99 under Section 550 of the Bankruptcy Code;

B) For costs of suit incurred herein, including, without limitation, attorneys' fees;

C) For pre- and post-judgment interest on the judgment amount to the fullest extent allowed by applicable law; and

D) all such other and further relief as the Court may deem just and proper.

Dated: January 12, 2014

Respectfully submitted,

By: *_/s/ Peter Smith_*
PETER SMITH, ESQ. (DE Bar No. 1100)
Laurel, Harry & Moser, LLP
999 Livestreet Road
Wilmington, DE 16666
Tel: 333-333-3214
Email: ps@laurelharrymoser.com

Counsel for the Plaintiff

To:

William Brown, Esq.
The Law Office of William Brown
1990 Law Street
Wilmington, DE 19806
Tel: 333-555-5555
Email: wbrown@wblaw.com

and

Brown Smith, Esq.
Brown LLP
99 South End Street
99th Floor
New York, NY
Tel: 666-999-9999
Email: bs@brownlaw.com

Counsels to the Defendant

CHAPTER 7

Bibliography

8.1 Law Journal Articles

Abrams, Gregory S., Joseph L. Steinfeld Jr., & Joseph A. Hess, *Prosecuting Preference Actions Post-BAPCPA: Another View Toward a Reliable Statistical Model*. 25-10 ABI J. 54 (2006)

Ahart, Alan M. *The Limited Scope of Implied Powers of a Bankruptcy Judge: A Statutory Court of Bankruptcy, Not a Court of Equity*. 79 Am. Bankr. L.J. 1 (2005)

Bachrach, George J. & Cynthia E. Rodgers-Waire. *The Surety's Rights to the Contract Funds in the Principal's Chapter 11 Bankruptcy Case*. 35 Tort & Ins. L.J. 1 (1999)

Baum, Kevin M. Note: *Apparently, "No Good Deed Goes Unpunished"*: The Earmarking Doctrine, Equitable Subrogation, and Inquiry Notice Are Necessary Protections When Refinancing Consumer Mortgages in an Uncertain Credit Market,** Chase Manhattan Mortgage Corp. v. Shapiro (In re Lee), *530 F.3d 458, 475 (6th Cir. 2008) (Merritt, J., dissenting)."* 83 St. John's L. Rev. 1361 (2009)

Bernstein, Stan, Susan H. Seabury, & Jack F. Williams, *Squaring Bankruptcy Valuation Practice with Daubert Demands*. 16 Am. Bankr. Inst. L. Rev. 161 (2008)

Bogart, Daniel B. *Finding the Still Small Voice: The Liability of Bankruptcy Trustees and the Work of the National Bankruptcy Review Commission*. 102 Dick. L. Rev. 703 (1998)

Carlson, David Gray & William H. Widen. *The Earmarking Defense to Voidable Preference Liability: A Reconceptualization*. 73 Am. Bankr. L.J. 591 (1999

Clark, Stephen. *Insider Trading and Financial Economics: Where Do We Go from Here?* 16 Stan. J.L. Bus. & Fin. 43 (2010)

Countryman, Vern. *Bankruptcy Preferences—Current Law and Proposed Changes*. 11 U.C.C. L.J. 95 (1978)

Countryman, Vern. *The Concept of a Voidable Preference in Bankruptcy*. 38 Vand. L. Rev. 713 (1985)

Fisher, Mark. *7th Circ. Provides Road Map for Preference Defendants*. Law360, https://www.law360.com/ articles/811325/7th-circ-provides-road-map-for-preference-defendants (June 27, 2016)

Fortgang & King, *The 1978 Bankruptcy Code: Some Wrong Policy Decisions*. 56 N.Y.U. L. Rev. 1148 (1981)

Goldstein, Brian S. *Recent Development in Bankruptcy Law: Preferences and Setoff*. 1 Bank. Dev. J. 356 (1984)

Gotberg, Brook E. *Conflicting Preferences in Business Bankruptcy: The Need for Different Rules in Different Chapters*. 100 Iowa L. Rev. 51 (2014)

Hall, Beverly J. *Recent Developments in Bankruptcy Law: Preferences and Setoffs: Sections 547 and 553*. 2 Bank. Dev. J. 49 (1985)

Hensley, William M. *Worlds in Collision: Mechanic's Liens and Federal Bankruptcy Schemes Confront Each Other and How the Courts Reconcile the Conflict*. 31 Whittier L. Rev. 621 (2010)

Herbert, Michael J. *The Trustee Versus the Trade Creditor II: The 1984 Amendment to Section 547(c)(2) of the Bankruptcy Code*. 2 Bank. Dev. J. 201 (1985)

Bibliography

Hollander, Evan C. *Recent Development: Preferences: Section 547.* 3 Bank. Dev. J. 365 (1986)

Klee, Kenneth N. & K. John Shaffer, *Chapter 11 Issues: Creditors' Committees Under Chapter 11 of the Bankruptcy Code.* 44 S.C. L. Rev. 995 (1993)

Kotliar, Brian. Note: *A New Reading of the Ordinary Course of Business Exception in Section 547(c)(2).* 21 Am. Bankr. Inst. L. Rev. 211 (2013)

Kraus, Bruce R. Note, *Preferential Transfers and the Value of the Insolvent Firm.* 87 Yale L. J. 1449 (1978)

Leal, Manuel D. *Discovery Under Bankruptcy Procedure: A "Trap Door?"* 84 N.D. L. Rev. 111 (2008)

Lipson, Jonathan C. *The Shadow Bankruptcy System.* 89 B.U. L. Rev. 1609 (2009)

Lomax, Lisa A. *Alternative Dispute Resolution in Bankruptcy: Rule 9019 and Bankruptcy Mediation Programs.* 68 Am. Bankr. L.J. 55 (1994)

Mabey, Ralph R., Charles J. Tabb, & Ira S. Dizengoff. *Expanding the Reach of Alternative Dispute Resolution in Bankruptcy: The Legal and Practical Bases for the Use of Mediation and the Other Forms of ADR.* 46 S.C. L. Rev. 1259 (1995)

Markus, Ilan. *The Correct Application of Section 547(e)(3): Deciding Whether Wage Garnishment Transfers Are Preferential.* 12 Bank. Dev. J. 219 (1995)

McCoid, John C., II, *Bankruptcy, Preferences, and Efficiency: An Expression of Doubt.* 67 Va. L. Rev. 249 (1981)

McCullough, Elizabeth H. *Bankruptcy Trustee Liability: Is There a Method in the Madness?* 15 Lewis & Clark L. Rev. 153 (2011)

McKenzie, Troy A. *Judicial Independence, Autonomy, and the Bankruptcy Courts.* 62 Stan. L. Rev. 747 (2010)

Miller, Harvey R. *The Changing Face of Chapter 11: A Reemergence of the Bankruptcy Judge as Producer, Director, and Sometimes Star of the Reorganization Passion Play.* 69 Am. Bankr. L.J. 431 (1995)

Nickles, Steve H. *Behavioral Effect of New Bankruptcy Law on Management and Lawyers: Collage of Recent Statutes and Cases Discouraging Chapter 11 Bankruptcy.* 59 Ark. L. Rev. 329 (2006)

Ontko, David A. *Ordinary Business Terms Must Not Be Ignored: The [F]orgotten But Critical Role of § 547(c)(2)(c) in the Ordinary Course of Business Exception to the Preference Rules.* 6 Bank. Dev. J. 429 (1989)

Pardo, Rafael I. *On Proof of Preferential Effect.* 55 Ala. L. Rev. 281 (2004)

Petrovski, Novica. LL.M. thesis: *The Bankruptcy Code, Section 1121: Exclusivity Reloaded.* 11 Am. Bankr. Inst. L. Rev. 451 (2003)

Ponoroff, Lawrence & Julie C. Ashby. *Desperate Times and Desperate Measures: The Troubled State of the Ordinary Course of Business Defense – and What to Do About It.* 72 Wash. L. Rev. 5 (1997)

Ponoroff, Lawrence. *BAPCPA AT TEN: Bankruptcy Preferences: Recalcitrant Passengers Aboard the Flight from Creditor Equality.* 90 Am. Bankr. L.J. 329 (2016)

Ponoroff, Lawrence. *Evil Intentions and An Irresolute Endorsement for Scientific Rationalism: Bankruptcy Preferences One More Time.* 1993 Wis. L. Rev. 1439 (1993)

Quinn, Harris P. *The Subsequent New Value Exception Under Section 547(c)(4) of the Bankruptcy Code—Judicial Gloss is Creditors' Loss.* 24 Mem. St. U. L. Rev. 667 (1994)

Rafael I. Pardo and Kathryn A. Watts, *The Structural Exceptionalism of Bankruptcy Administration,* 60 UCLA L. Rev. 384 (2012

Rapoport, Nancy B. *Seeing the Forest* and *the Trees: The Proper Role of the Bankruptcy Attorney.* 70 Ind. L.J. 783 (1995).

Rapoport, Nancy B. *The Case for Value Billing in Chapter 11.* 7 J. Bus. & Tech. L. 117 (2011)

Roe, Mark J. & Frederick Tung. *Breaking Bankruptcy Priority: How Rent-Seeking Upends the Creditors' Bargain.* 99 Va. L. Rev. 1235 (2013)

Bibliography

Ross, Thomas. *The Impact of Section 547 of the Bankruptcy Code upon Secured and Unsecured Creditors.* 69 Minn. L. Rev. 39 (1984)

Sanborn, Nancy L. Note: *Avoidance Recoveries in Bankruptcy: For the Benefit of the Estate or the Secured Creditor?* 90 Colum. L. Rev. 1376 (1990)

Sears, Nick. *Defeating the Preference System: Using the Subsequent New Value Defense and Administrative Expense Claims to "Double Dip."* 28 Emory Bankr. Dev. J. 593 (2012)

Solomon, Spencer D. *Bankruptcy Best Practices from the Bench and Bar: Keeping Things In-House: Increasing Scrutiny of the Chapter 7 Trustee's Selection of Counsel.* 55 S. Tex. L. Rev. 665 (2014)

Tabb, Charles Jordan. *Panglossian Preference Paradigm?* 5 Am. Bankr. Inst. L. Rev. 407 (1997)

Thorne, Deborah L. *Lien on Me:, [sic] Reexamining the Ordinary Course Defense: A Multifactor Approach.* 32-11 ABI J. 32 (2013)

Vazzana, Bethaney J. *Trustee Recovery of Indirect Benefits Under Section 547(b) of the Bankruptcy Code.* 6 Bank. Dev. J. 403 (1989)

Weisberg, Robert. *Commercial Morality, the Merchant Character, and the History of the Voidable Preference.* 39 Stan. L. Rev. 3, 12 (1986)

Woodward, William J., Jr.. *ADR Meets Bankruptcy: Cross-Purposes or Cross-Pollination?: The Third Way: Mediation of Products Claims in the Piper Aircraft Trust.* 17 Am. Bankr. Inst. L. Rev. 463 (2009)

Woodward, William J., Jr.. *Evaluating Bankruptcy Mediation.* 1999 J. Disp. Resol. 1 (1999)

8.2   Books

Churchill, Winston. Address Before the House of Commons (Nov. 11, 1947), in *Winston S Churchill: His Complete Speeches 1897-1963*. Robert Rhodes James ed., 1974

Gilmore, Grant. *Security Interests in Personal Property* § 8.3. 1965

Stein, Sol. *Bankruptcy: A Feast for Lawyers*. New York: M. Evans, 1992

5-547 *Collier on Bankruptcy* 547.03[2][a] (16th ed. 2016)

5-547 *Collier on Bankruptcy* 547.04[4][a] (16th ed. 2016)

5-547 *Collier on Bankruptcy* 547.04[2][a][ii] (16th ed. 2016)

5-547 *Collier on Bankruptcy* 547.04[2][a][iii] (16th ed. 2016)

5-547 *Collier on Bankruptcy* 547.04[4] (16th ed. 2016)

5-547 *Collier on Bankruptcy* 547.11[6] (16th ed. 2016)

5-547 *Collier on Bankruptcy* 547.13 (16th. 2016)

5-550 *Collier on Bankruptcy* 550.02[4][a] (16th ed. 2016)

Collier on Bankruptcy App. Pt. 4(c) at 48 (16th ed. 2017)

8.3 Statutes

7 U.S.C. §§ 181-231

7 U.S.C. § 499(a)

7 U.S.C. § 499(c)(3)

11 U.S.C. § 101(10)

11 U.S.C. § 105(d)

11 U.S.C. § 109

11 U.S.C. § 1102

11 U.S.C. § 1121

11 U.S.C. § 327(a)

11 U.S.C. § 328(a)

11 U.S.C. § 365

11 U.S.C. § 365(c)

11 U.S.C. § 521

11 U.S.C. § 546(c)

11 U.S.C. § 546(c)(1)

11 U.S.C. § 546(c)(1)(B)

11 U.S.C. § 546(c)(A)

11 U.S.C. § 547

11 U.S.C. § 547(b)

11 U.S.C. § 547(b)(4)

11 U.S.C. § 547(b)(5)

11 U.S.C. § 547(b)(5)(A)

11 U.S.C. § 547(c)

11 U.S.C. § 547(c)(1)

11 U.S.C. § 547(c)(2)

11 U.S.C. § 547(c)(4)

11 U.S.C. § 547(d)

11 U.S.C. § 547(f)

11 U.S.C. § 704

15 U.S.C. § 78

8.4   Procedural Rules

Fed. R. Bankr. P. 7004

Fed. R. Bankr. P. 7008

Fed. R. Bankr. P. 7012

Fed. R. Bankr. P. 7016

Fed. R. Bankr. P. 7026

Fed. R. Bankr. P. 7033

Fed. R. Bankr. P. 7034

Fed. R. Bankr. P. 7036

Fed. R. Bankr. P. 7056

Fed. R. Bankr. P. 9003(a)

Fed. R. Bankr. P. 9014(a)

Fed. R. Bankr. P. 9019(a)

Fed. R. Civ. P. 16(b)

Fed. R. Civ. P. 16(b)(3)(B)(iv)

Fed. R. Civ. P. 26(f)

Fed. R. Civ. P. 33

Fed. R. Civ. P. 34

Fed. R. Civ. P. 36

Fed. R. Civ. P. 36(a)(4)

Fed. R. Civ. P. 36(b)

Fed. R. Civ. P. 56

8.5 Cases

Adams v. Anderson (*In re* Superior Stamp & Coin Co., Inc.), 223 F.3d 1004, 44 C.B.C. 2d 1382 (9th Cir. 2000)

Advo-System, Inc. v. Maxway Corp., 37 F.3d 1044 (4th Cir. 1994)

Alvarado v. Walsh (*In re* LCO Enterprises), 12 F.3d 938 (9th Cir. 1993)

American States Inc. Co. v. Glover Constr. Co. (*In re* Glover Constr. Co., Inc.), 30 B.R. 873 (Bankr. W.D. Ky. 1983)

Ames Merch. Corp. v. Cellmark Paper Inc. (Ames Dep't Stores, Inc.), 450 B.R. 24 (Bankr. S.D.N.Y. 2011)

Barash v. Public Fin. Corp., 658 F.2d 504 (7th Cir. 1981)

Barnes v. Karbank Holdings, LLC (In re JS & RB, Inc.), 446 B.R. 350 (Bankr. W.D. Mo. 2011)

Bender Shipbuilding and Repair Co. v. Oil Recovery Co. Inc. of Alabama (*In re* Bender Shipbuilding and Repair Co.), 479 B.R. 899 (Bankr. S.D. Ala. 2012)

Bob Grissett Golf Shoppes, Inc., 34 B.R. 320 (Bankr. E.D. Va. (1983)

Boberschmidt v. Society Nat'l Bank (*In re* Jones), 226 F.3d 917 (7th Cir. 2000)

Bonded Fin. Servs., Inc. v. European Am. Bank, 838 F.2d 890 (7th Cir. 1988)

Boone v. Marlatt (*In re* Day Telecommunications, Inc.), 70 B.R. 904 (Bankr. E.D.N.C. 1987)

Branch v. Ropes & Gray (*In re* Bank of New England Corp.), 161 B.R. 557, 24 Bankr. Ct. Dec. (CRR) 1621 (Bankr. D. Mass. 1993)

Brandt v. Samuel, Son & Co., Ltd. (*In re* Longview Aluminum, L.L.C.), Case No. 03 B 12184, 2005 Bankr. LEXIS 1312 (Bankr. N.D. Ill. 2005)

Brothers Gourmet Coffees, Inc. v. Armenia Coffee Corp. (*In re* Brothers Gourmet Coffees, Inc.), 271 B.R. 456 (Bankr. D. Del. 2002)

Burch v. Bonded Adjusters, Inc. (*In re* Estates of Pelc), 34 B.R. 823 (Bankr. D. Or. 1983)

Burtch v. Opus, LLC (*In re* Opus East, LLC), 528 B.R. 30 (Bankr. D. Del. 2015)

Bibliography

Burtch v. Texstars, Inc. (*In re* AE Liquidation, Inc.), 70 C.B.C. 2d 755, 2013 Bankr. LEXIS 4144 (Bankr. D. Del. 2013)

Canadian Pac. Forest Prods. Ltd. v. J.D. Irving, Ltd. (*In re* Gibson Group, Inc.), 66 F.3d 1436 (6th Cir. 1995)

Central Hardware Co. v. Sherwin-Williams Co. (*In re* Spirit Holding Co., Inc.), 153 F.3d 902 (8th Cir. 1998)

Claybrook v. Consolidated Foods, Inc. (*In re* Bake-Line Grp., LLC), 359 B.R. 566 (Bankr. D. Del. 2007)

Cohen v. Kern (*In re* Kennesaw Mint, Inc.), 32 B.R. 799 (Bankr. N.D. Ga. 1983)

Coral Petroleum, Inc. v. Banque Paribas-London, 797 F.2d 1351 (5th Cir. 1986)

Cox v. Momar Inc. (*In re* Affiliated Foods Southwest Inc.), 750 F.3d 714 (8th Cir. 2014)

Davis v. Clarklift West, Inc. (*In re* Quebecor World (USA), Inc.), 518 B.R. 757 (Bankr. S.D.N.Y. 2014)

Davis v. R.A. Brooks Trucking Co., Inc. (*In re* Quebecor World (USA), Inc.), 491 B.R. 379 (Bankr. S.D.N.Y. 2013)

Dill v. Brad Hall & Assocs., Inc. (*In re* Indian Capitol Distrib.), No. 7-09-11558 SA, 2012 Bankr. LEXIS 3725 (Bankr. D. N.M. 2012)

East Coast Potato Distributors v. Grant (*In re* Super Spud, Inc.), 77 B.R. 930 (Bankr. M.D. Fla. 1987)

Ellenberg v. Tulip Prod. Polymerics, Inc. (*In re* T.B. Home Sewing Enters., Inc.), 173 B.R. 782 (Bankr. N.D. Ga. 1993)

Excel Enterprises, Inc. v. Sikes, Gardes & Co. (*In re* Excel Enterprises, Inc.), 83 B.R. 427 (Bankr. W.D. La. 1988)

Fiber Lite Corp. v. Molded Acoustical Prods., Inc. (*In re* Molded Acoustical Prods., Inc.), 18 F.3d. 217 (3d Cir. 1994)

First Nat'l Bank of Barnesville v. Rafoth (*In re* Baker & Getty Fin. Servs., Inc.), 974 F.2d 712, 27 C.B.C. 2d 1112 (6th Cir. 1992)

First Nat'l Bank of Danville, Ill. v. Phalen, 62 F.2d 21 (7th Cir. 1932)

G.H. Leidenheimer Baking Co., Ltd. v. Sharp (*In re* SGSM Acquisition Co., LLC), 439 F.3d 233 (5th Cir. 2006)

Gasmark Ltd. Liquidating Trust v. Louis Dreyfus Natural Gas Corp., 158 F.3d 312 (5th Cir. 1998)

Gonzales v. Sun Life Ins. Co. (*In re* Furr's Supermakets, Inc.), 485 B.R. 672 (Bankr. D. N.M. 2012)

Goodman v. Candy Fleet, LLC (*In re* Gulf Fleet Holdings), 2014 Bankr. LEXIS 1123 (Bankr. W.D. La. 2014)

Grant v. Suntrust Bank, Central Florida, N.A. (*In re* L. Bee Furniture Co., Inc.), 203 B.R. 778 (Bankr. M.D. Fla. 1996)

Grogan v. Liberty Nat'l Life Ins. Co. (*In re* Advance Glove Mfg. Co.), 761 F.2d 249 (6th Cir. 1985)

Grogan v. Southwest Textiles, Inc. (*In re* Advance Glove Mfg. Co.), 42 B.R. 489 (Bankr. E.D. Mich. 1984)

Gropper v. Unitrac, S.A. (*In re* Fabric Buys of Jericho, Inc.), 33 B.R. 334 (Bankr. S.D.N.Y. 1983)

Grubb v. General Contract Purchase Corp., 94 F.2d 70 (2d Cir. 1938)

Gulf City Seafoods, Inc. v. Ludwig Shrimp Co. (*In re* Gulf City Seafoods, Inc.), 296 F.3d 363 (5th Cir. 2002)

Gull Air, Inc. v. Beech Acceptance Corp., Inc. (*In re* Gull Air, Inc.), 82 B.R. 1 (Bankr. D. Mass. 1988)

Hansen v. MacDonald Meat Co. (*In re* Kemp Pacific Fisheries, Inc.), 16 F.3d 313 (9th Cir. 1994)

Harstad v. First Am. Bank, 39 F.2d 898 (8th Cir. 1994)

Hechinger Inv. Co. of Del., Inc. v. Universal Forest Prods., Inc. (In re Hechinger Inv. Co. of Delaware, Inc.), 489 F.3d 568 (3d Cir. 2007)

Hitachi Denshi Amer., Ltd. v. Rozel Indus., Inc. (*In re* Rozel Indus., Inc.), 74 B.R. 643 (Bankr. N.D. Ill. 1987)

In re Arctic Air Conditioning, Inc., 35 B.R. 107 (Bankr. E.D. Tenn. 1983

Bibliography

In re Economy Milling Co., Inc., 37 B.R. 914 (D. S.C. 1983)

In re Forklift LP Corp., 2006 US Dist. Lexis 50264

In re Fresh Approach, Inc., 51 B.R. 412 (Bankr. N.D. Tex. 1985)

In re Georgia Steel, Inc., 38 B.R. 829 (Bankr. M.D. Ga. 1984)

In re Middendorf, 381 B.R. 774, (Bankr. D. Kan. 2008)

In re Morton Shoe Companies, Inc., 36 Bankr. 320, 9 B.C.D. 654 (Bankr. D. Mass. 1983).

In re Piper Aircraft Corp., 162 B.R. 619 (Bankr. S.D. Fla. 1994)

In re R.H. Macy & Co., Nos. 92 B 40477-40486 (Bankr. S.D.N.Y. 1994)

In re Superior Toy & Mfg. Co., Inc., 78 F.3d 1169 (7th Cir. 1996)

In re Tolona Pizza Prods. Corp., 3 F.3d 1029 (7th Cir. 1993)

Jensen v. Raymond Bldg. Supply Corp. (*In re* Homes of Port Charlotte Florida, Inc.), 109 B.R. 489 (Bankr. M.D. Fla. 1990)

John Deere Indus. Equip. Co. v. Southern Equip Sales Co., Inc. (*In re* Southern Equip. Sales Co., Inc.), 24 B.R. 788 (Bankr. D. N.J. 1982)

John Mitchell, Inc. v. Steinbrugge (*In re* Hanna), 72 F.3d 114 (9th Cir. 1995)

Kapila v. Media Buying, Inc. (*In re* Ameri P.O.S., Inc.), 355 B.R. 876 (Bankr. S.D. Fla. 2006)

Kimmelman v. Port Auth. of N.Y. and N.J. (*In re* Kiwi Int'l Air Lines, Inc.), 344 F.3d 311 (3d Cir. 2003)

Lawson v. Ford Motor Co. (*In re* Roblin Indus., Inc.), 78 F.3d 30 (2d Cir. 1996)

Lids Corp. v. Marathon Investment Partners, L.P. (*In re* Lids Corp.), 281 B.R. 535 (Bankr. D. Del. 2002)

Lightfoot v. Amelia Maritime Servs., Inc. (*In re* Sea Bridge Marine, Inc.), 412 B.R. 868 (Bankr. E.D. La. 2008)

Logan v. Basic Distrib. Corp. (*In re* Fred Hawes Org., Inc.), 957 F.2d 239 (6th Cir. 1992)

Lubman v. C.A. Guard Masonry Contr., Inc. (*In re* Gem Constr. Corp. of Va.), 262 B.R. 638 (Bankr. E.D. Va. 2000)

Lucas Aerospace, Inc. v. Continental Airlines, Inc. (*In re* Continental Airlines, Inc.), 171 B.R. 187 (Bankr. D. Del. 1994)

Marathon Oil Co. v. Flatau (*In re* Craig Oil Co.), 785 F.2d 1563 (11th Cir. 1986)

McCarthy v. Navistar Fin. Corp. (*In re* Vogel Van & Storage, Inc.), 210 B.R. 27 (N.D.N.Y. 1997)

McClendon v. Cal-Wood Door (In re Wadsworth Bldg. Components, Inc.), 711 F.2d 122 (9th Cir. 1983)

Mendelsohn v. Gordon (*In re* Who's Who Worldwide Registry, Inc.), 197 B.R. 193 (Bankr. E.D.N.Y. 1996)

Mid-Atlantic Supply, Inc. of Virginia v. Three Rivers Aluminum Co. (*In re* Mid Atlantic Supply Co.), 790 F.2d 1121 (4th Cir. 1986)

Mitsui Mfrs. Bank v. Unicom Computer Corp. (*In re* Unicom Computer Corp.), 13 F.3d 321 (9th Cir. 1994)

Modern Metal Prods. Co. v. Virtual Engineering, Inc. (*In re* Modern Metal Prods. Co.), 2015 Bankr. LEXIS 1188 (Bankr. N.D. Ill. 2015)

Moltech Power Sys. v. Tooh Dineh Indus., Inc. (*In re* Moltech Power Sys., Inc.), 327 B.R. 675 (Bankr. N.D. Fla. 2005)

National Bank of Newport v. National Herkimer Cty. Bank of Little Falls, 225 U.S. 178, 32 S. Ct. 633, 56 L. Ed. 1042 (1912)

New York Cty. Nat'l Bank v. Massey, 192 U.S. 138 (1901)

O'Rourke v. Coral Constr., Inc. (*In re* E.R. Fegert, Inc.), 88 B.R. 258 (9th Cir. BAP 1988)

Official Unsecured Creditors Committee of Sufolla, Inc. v. U.S. Nat'l Bank of Oregon (*In re* Sufolla, Inc.), 2 F.3d 977 (9th Cir. 1993)

Pereira v. United Parcel Service of America, Inc. a/k/a UPS (*In re* Waterford Wedgewood USA, Inc.), 508 B.R. 821 (Bankr. S.D.N.Y. 2014)

Pettigrew v. Trust Co. Bank (*In re* Bishop), 17 B.R. 180 (1982)

Pfau v. First Nat'l Bank (*In re* Schmidt), 26 B.R. 89 (Bankr. D. Minn. 1982)

Pine Top Ins. Co. v. Bank of Am. Nat'l Trust & Savs. Assoc., 969 F.2d 321 (7th Cir. 1992)

PN Chapter 11 Estate Liquidating Trust v. Inserts East, Inc. (*In re* Philadelphia Newspapers, LLC), 468 B.R. 712 (Bankr. E.D. Pa. 2012)

Post-Confirmation Comm. v. Tomball Forest, Ltd. (*In re* Bison Bldg. Holdings, Inc.), 473 B.R. 168 (Bankr. S.D. Tex. 2012)

Reynolds v. Commissioner of Internal Revenue, 861 F.2d 469 (6th Cir. 1988)

Rushton v. E & S Int'l Enters., Inc. (*In re* Eleva, Inc.), 235 B.R. 486 (B.A.P. 10th Cir. 1999)

Schwinn Plan Comm. v. Transamerica Ins. Fin. Corp. (*In re* Schwinn Bicycle Co.), 200 B.R. 980 (Bankr. N.D. Ill. 1996)

Shodeen v. Airline Software, Inc. (*In re* Accessair, Inc.), 314 B.R. 386 (B.A.P. 8th Cir. 2004)

Silverman Consulting, Inc. v. Canfor Wood Prods. Mktg. (In re Payless Cashways, Inc.), 306 B.R. 243 (B.A.P. 8th Cir. 2004

Simon v. Gerdau MacSteel, Inc. (*In re* American Camshaft Specialties, Inc.), 444 B.R. 347 (Bankr. E.D. Mich. 2011)

Simon v. Gerdau MacSteel, Inc. (*In re* Camshaft Specialties, Inc.), 444 B.R. 347 (Bankr. E.D. Mich. 2011)

Smith v. Creative Fin. Mgmt., Inc. (*In re* Virginia-Carolina Fin. Corp.), 954 F.2d 193 (4th Cir. 1992)

Sparkman v. Martin Marietta Materials, Inc. (*In re* Mainline Contracting, Inc.), 68 C.B.C. 2d 736, 2012 Bankr. LEXIS 4986 (Bankr. E.D.N.C. 2012)

Springel v. Prosser (*In re* Prosser), 2009 Bankr. LEXIS 3209 (Bankr. D. V.I. 2009)

Suhar v. Agree Auto Servs., Inc. (In re Blakely), 497 B.R. 267 (Bankr. N.D. Ohio 2013)

Tidwell v. Galbreath (*In re* Galbreath), 207 B.R. 309 (Bankr. M.D. Ga. 1997)

Tomlins v. BRW Paper Co., Inc. (*In re* Tulsa Litho Co.), 229 B.R. 806 (B.A.P. 10th Cir. 1999)

Toshiba Am., Inc. v. Video King of Illinois, Inc. (*In re* Video King of Ill., Inc.), 100 B.R. 1008 (Bankr. N.D. Ill. 1989)

Trans World Airlines, Inc. v. Travellers Int'l AG. (*In re* Trans World Airlines, Inc.), 180 B.R. 389 (Bankr. D. Del. 1994)

U.S. Bank Nat'l Ass'n v. Spectra Mktg. Sys. (*In re* Interstate Bakeries Corp.), Nos. 04-45814, 09-4177, 2011 Bankr. LEXIS 140 (Bankr. W.D. Mo. 2011)

Union Carbide Corp. v. Newboles, 686 F.2d 593 (7th Cir. 1982)

United Rentals, Inc. v. Angell, 592 F.3d 525 (4th Cir. 2010)

United Student Aid Funds, Inc. v. Espinosa, 559 U.S. 260 (2010)

Unsecured Creds. Comm. v. Jason's Foods, Inc. (*In re* Sparrer Sausage Co., Inc.), 2014 Bankr. LEXIS 3661 (Bankr. N.D. Ill. 2014)

Velde v. Kirsch, 543 F.3d 469 (8th Cir. 2008)

Webster v. Management Network Group, Inc. (*In re* Nettel Corp., Inc.), 364 B.R. 433 (Bankr. D. D.C. 2006)

Weinman v. Allison Payment Sys., LLC (*In re* Centrix Fin., LLC), 434 B.R. 880 (Bankr. D. Colo. 2010)

Western Tie and Timber Co. v. Brown, 196 U.S. 502 (1905)

Willson v. McPhersons Partnership (*In re* Central Louisiana Grain Cooperative, Inc.), 497 B.R. 229 (Bankr. W.D. La. 2013)

Wolkowitz v. American Research Corp. (*In re* DAK Industries, Inc.), 170 F.3d 1197 (9th Cir. 1999)

Writing Sales Ltd. Partnership v. Pilot Corp. of Am. (*In re* Writing Sales Ltd. Partnership), 96 B.R. 175 (Bankr. E.D. Wis. 1989)

Yurika Foods Corp. v. United Parcel Serv. (*In re* Yurika Foods Corp.), 888 F.2d 42 (6th Cir. 1989)

Zachman Homes, Inc. v. Oredson (*In re* Zachman Homes, Inc.), 40 B.R. 171 (Bankr. D. Minn. 1984)

8.6 Other

17 C.F.R. § 240.10b-5

H.R. REP. No. 595, 95th Cong., 1st Sess. (1977)

Johnson, William B. *Timing of Transfer as Being in "Ordinary Course of Business or Financial Affairs" for Purposes of 11 U.S.C.A. § 547(c)(2)(A) -- Chapter 7 Cases.* 75 A.L.R. Fed. 2d 93

Pub. L. 95-598, 92 Stat. 2549, November 6, 1978

About the Author

Roland Gary Jones, Esq.

Mr. Jones has practiced bankruptcy law for over two decades. His primary focus is representing corporate defendants in preference and fraudulent conveyance litigation. Mr. Jones has represented clients in bankruptcy courts nationwide and has a national client base. He has also represented clients based in Europe and the Far East.

While defending clawback cases in major bankruptcies such as Madoff Investment Securities, Enron Energy Services, TWA Airlines, General Motors, Ames Department Stores and Furniture Brands International, Mr. Jones represented clients such as FedEx, Victoria's Secret, JetBlue, and Colgate-Palmolive.

In addition to his law practice, Mr. Jones has authored professional articles on bankruptcy issues for the New York Law Journal, The Environmental Claims Journal, The Mergers and Acquisitions Report, and other scholarly publications. Mr. Jones also edits and writes the Clawback Report, a monthly newsletter on clawback topics.

Mr. Jones has also produced a series of introductory videos on preferences and fraudulent conveyances topics available for Continuing Legal Education credits in New York and other states. These videos are available for viewing at www.rolandjones.com.

Mr. Jones was the founding member and former Chair of the Federal Bar Association Empire State Chapter Bankruptcy Committee. The Bankruptcy Committee has hosted experts to speak on topics relevant to both bankruptcy and non-bankruptcy practitioners. Guest speakers have included The Honorable Jerrold Nadler on new bankruptcy legislation, Wilbur L. Ross, Jr. of Rothschild Inc. on the distressed bond market, and Professor Edward Altman of New York University on bankruptcy investing.

As the founding member and current President of the National Association of Bankruptcy Litigators (NABL), Mr. Jones organized the first association devoted primarily to clawback litigation. The NABL consist currently of 110 bankruptcy clawback attorneys.

Mr. Jones' introduction to bankruptcy practice began by serving as a judicial law clerk to Chief U.S. Bankruptcy Judge Conrad B. Duberstein of the Eastern District of New York during law school. He continued his training after graduation by clerking for U.S. Bankruptcy Judge Cecilia H. Goetz of the Eastern District of New York from 1990 to 1991.

Mr. Jones attended the Horace Mann School, Columbia University (B.A. Ancient Studies) and Brooklyn Law School (J.D. 1990). He is admitted to practice law before the United States District Courts for the Southern and Eastern Districts of New York, as well as the United States Court of Appeals for the Second Circuit.

Mr. Jones was born in New York City.

Roland Gary Jones, Esq.
Jones & Associates
1745 Broadway, 17th Floor
New York, NY 10019
Tel. No.: (347) 862-9254 Ext. 701
Fax: (212) 202-4416
rgj@rolandjones.com
www.rolandjones.com
LinkedIn: www.linkedin.com/in/rgj59/

Made in the USA
Columbia, SC
04 November 2020